The Interdimensional Self
The Way to Peace

Messages from
Jeshua ben Joseph (Jesus)

Jeshua
The Personal Christ
Volume IV

ISBN 1-878555-14-6

Published by
Oakbridge University Press

www.Oakbridge.org
Judith@Oakbridge.org

*Heartfelt thanks to all, seen and unseen,
who have assisted in the preparation
of this book.*

A special thanks to Ted Meske

Contents

Foreword

In the spring of 2003, I visited a community in Florida to talk about the final book in a series of books I had written in the name of Jesus (the books of *A Course of Love*). It was one of my first presentations and Jesus had asked me not to prepare. Jesus' words came to me in written form, and unlike Judith Coates, I had little experience as a public speaker. Although not preparing was hard for me, I understood why Jesus wanted me to just be myself and be in dialogue with people. To be ourselves, our true selves, and to live (and speak) from that true place is the aim toward which Jesus draws us in Judith's work as well as my own.

And so, on the day of my presentation, I addressed a small audience as "myself" and as "myself" spoke briefly of the difficult time I had with being in this unusual position of hearing and recording and now representing the words of Jesus. After my Florida dialogue, Marcia Bond, a lovely woman well acquainted with Judith and her books, gave me Volume I of *The Personal Christ* and told me that I really ought to talk to Judith. While she stated her intention as "getting together" those of us who were doing this work, I felt that she also recognized my human need for the reassurance that comes of "professional" companionship.

As I drove home to Minnesota I opened *The Personal Christ* in my motel room. Tears came to my eyes. I wondered why what Judith had presented in *The Personal Christ* felt so nurturing, so loving, so gentle while what I had written in *A Course of Love* felt so much more like a course, dense paragraphs and chapters that had felt difficult to receive and to understand. It wasn't that they, too, weren't loving and gentle. It was just that on that night I was weary, and the personal

Christ, the Christ who spoke to me as a friend might talk to me over a cup of coffee, was the Christ I needed.

Thus began my association with Judith's work.

Not long afterwards, due to Marcia's thoughtfulness, Judith and I began to talk with one another.

Although I had many spiritual soul mates, I had no one I could talk to who fulfilled a role so similar to my own. I had so many questions I wanted to ask. I wanted to know if Judith felt any of the unease that I did. I was curious about how she handled various situations. Our first conversation, a conversation between two total strangers, was very personal, almost like one you might imagine having with a friend at work, someone with whom you could complain about the difficulties of that work without sounding ungrateful for it, someone with whom you could also talk about the joy and the fulfillment of a common and personal passion. In that conversation, I knew Judith had felt what I had felt, experienced much of what I had experienced. It was a great solace to me to be able to enter dialogue with Judith. I appreciated her wise counsel.

As we turn to one another in conversation, just as when we turn to Jesus (Jeshua ben Joseph), more of who we are is revealed, and the personal Christ in us and in each other is revealed.

As we all seek to know more of who we are, Jeshua and Judith in this *Personal Christ* series and specifically in Volume IV, reveal a door, a door that encourages this precise knowing. What is the key to this door? "The willingness to believe, the willingness to say, 'There must be more than just this reality.'"

Jeshua, in expression through Judith, addresses the reader who has approached the doorway at which it is his or her time to say, "Perhaps there is much more to me."

With the intimacy of the spoken word, Judith Coates shares what has come to her from the Mind of God and extends Jeshua's invitation to us, an invitation to know that we, too, are not separate from the Mind of God.

This work moves the reader in gentle steps toward a willingness to embrace an expanded understanding of Self. What else could be more important? What else are we yearning for? Some of these steps, such as mindfulness, are common knowledge. Some, such as the instruction to "play" and to let our imaginations and even our desire guide us, are less common.

Always, Jeshua addresses each individual as his beloved, and the key component to Judith's work is that it enables the feeling of belovedness to reach each one of us. With our acceptance of our belovedness we can extend this belovedness to one another and begin to move into the time that has not yet been written, the time of a new consciousness.

We can do so in our weariness as well as in our wakefulness because of the intimacy of this one-on-one conversation. *The Personal Christ* is a lovely antidote to a world that so often feels impersonal and a realm of divinity that so often feels inaccessible.

— Mari Perron,

Author of *The Course of Love* Series

A Course of Love; The Treatises of A Course of Love; The Dialogues: Coming to Voice and The Grace Trilogy: Messages of Love, Grace, and Peace (Love, Book I, with Mary Kathryn Love and Julieanne Carver), and Peace, Book III.

The Interdimensional Self

Beloved one, I would speak with you now about your true Being, who you are and where you have come from. I would speak with you to answer many of the questions you have had about life, why you are here, and how you can see your life and circumstances more holy. I would speak with you about the love you have forgotten, and how you can remember.

Beloved one, what you do within this reality is a great miracle. You focus so intently and so specifically upon a reality that all of the rest of Reality—with a capital "R"—is momentarily forgotten. You focus most wondrously upon a time, a place, a personality, an individuality, a reality—small "r"—and yet at the same time you are functioning within other realities—small "r". You are having lifetimes in other realities, lifetimes as long as you can imagine and as short as you can imagine: living a whole lifetime in what would be in your measurement a nanosecond, and yet it is a lifetime full of experience within that spark of time.

Within your present reality the collective consciousness—the belief deeply embedded within you as the collective consciousness—says that there is but one reality. It is this "now" moment and you must attend to this reality. You must give it all of what you feel your energy to be. Within other realities there are belief systems which allow for the sampling of various venues of experience where you know you are having an experience —a lifetime within that dimension—and yet you know that you are also expressing and experiencing in other realities as well.

Now, within your current reality you have moved to a place of semi-remembrance of the Allness of You where you will allow that there is expanded consciousness with some of the brothers and sisters who do not have to have the focus upon the body; in other words, ones which you call the masters, the guides, the teachers, the angels, ones who are not activating the body. And you have built into your belief system a most wonderful door, a door which is opening now because you are decreeing that it is time for it to open, a door which is allowing your consciousness to know more of who you are.

You have dreamt many dreams, and you have dreamt dreams of awakening. That is where you stand now. You know that the awakening will happen--that is within your acceptance now--but there is still the belief in process which says it is yet to be; it is in the future somewhere. But within your belief system you have also put in the most wonderful door and a key to open that door, and you are in the process of turning the key and opening the door.

The key is a most wondrous one, and yet it is most simple. It is difficult for the ego, for the separated ego will not want that to be a part of your belief system. The key is the willingness to believe, the willingness to say, "There must be more than just this reality." It is that simple. You have been listening to the still small Voice within you which has been saying, "I am ready now to know Who I am. I am ready now to open the door and to walk through it into full realization and remembrance of Who I have always been and What I have always been from before time began."

So while you are yet miraculously and specifically focusing upon this reality, you are also building into this reality the open door which will allow you to move into the understanding and the experience of the interdimensional You. It also allows you to move into, have conversation with, the other you—plural—expressing in other dimensions.

Now, in times of meditation, in times when you allow the mind to be free of the constraints of the world, you have been daydreaming—most wondrous thing, the daydream—allowing the mind to go without judgment to wherever it would take you. You have gone to other realities and you have played; you have experienced what it feels like to be the most expansive star in the heavens. You have looked at the most wonderful lights in your heavens and you have known oneness with those lights. You have felt yourself blended, if you will, in the energy of the star, and you have moved beyond the perimeter of the small self.

As you have looked upon the most beautiful flower, you have glimpsed for an instant how it feels to be the energy of that flower; or how it feels to be as what you call within your concept the deva of that flower, the energy which guides, directs the growth and the expression of that flower; the same with a blade of grass, the same with a tree or a small, small seedling. You look at it and wonder at the miracle of life. You see amidst every creation the miracle of life everywhere.

You have allowed yourself from time to time to lose the sense of restriction which says, "I am only this individuality. I am only this body. I am only this personality." You have lost that small sense and expanded into knowing more of your true Self in what you would call dimensions even within this reality.

In times of meditation you have lost all sense of body. You have even lost all sense of mind. Then you have come back to this reality and someone may have asked of you, "Where have you been?" And you reply, "I didn't feel the passage of time. I don't know where I've been, but it felt good. It felt expansive. It felt like heaven. It felt wonderful." You try to find words to explain it and there are no words, for it is a knowing and a remembrance which goes beyond the restriction of this reality.

You play within many realities even as you would see a slice of time. You play within many realities that do not know or believe in the concept of time. You know how it feels to go as the flow of energy which is unrestricted. Within your concept in this reality you would call it the speed of light, because it is the fastest that you know or can imagine within this reality, and yet it is faster than light. It is beyond the concept of light.

You know how it feels to be one with the ocean of being. You know how it feels to experience the wholeness, the holiness, of you and the healing that you so desire. You have touched that place of great healing in times of meditation, in times of quiet. Allow the imagination to be free, to take you beyond what is known as this reality and then to release even the imagination and just *be*.

As you are beginning the process of connecting with the Allness which is you, use the tools that you have within this reality. You are the most wonderful makers of tools, of techniques. You are the ones who are creative in bringing forth the teachers who will speak to you of ways that will be as catalysts for remembrance. Use those tools in the beginning of this process. Already you have been doing that as you have been visiting many of the workshops, many of the speakers who have found themselves alive with an energy which goes beyond what you have known in everyday activity, and their energy has been so contagious that you have wanted to be in their presence. You have wanted to sit at their feet and to learn what they can impart to you.

You call forth these teachers because you are ready; you are desirous to know the next tool that you can use, the next catalyst for remembrance. You want to know more of your true Self. You want to come truly alive. You know that you can live the daily life, you can earn the golden coins enough to sustain the body, but there must be more to life. As you see your life rushing by—and all of you have felt an acceleration of time—you feel it rather incumbent upon you to get on with this search, not to waste any more time.

Now, in truth, you have never wasted any time, but the ego will speak to you, and sometimes there is the feeling that you have wasted time. You have explored many avenues, but now you are at a place where you want to know the tools; you want to know the process; you want to know the door and how to open it.

The door is within your understanding, your belief, even at this time. The key to opening it is the willingness to trust that you *can* open it, to trust that you *are* opening it; not to judge self, not to judge every revelation and to put it down, but to look upon every experience with awe and wonder and to praise self for what you are allowing yourself to experience, what you are allowing yourself to grasp as tools in the process.

Play with the tools which you create. Play with the tools of the process. Then sit with the revelations that those tools will present to you. Sit with the revelations and ask, "Where do these revelations take me?"

Allow yourself to be the magician who will put together various revelations, seemingly separate, and yet as you put them together the magician of you will make a new revelation, a new gestalt, if you will, out of all of the pieces of the revelations which have come before.

Then sit with that revelation and say, "If this be true, where does this take me?" Do not be afraid to claim where it will take you. Go boldly into new territory.

Do you know that is why you enjoy your science fiction programs so much? It is because you want to throw off restrictions of what this collective consciousness of reality has told you it has to be. And you, at the very depth of your being, have said, "No, there is more. There is much more. I vaguely, very vaguely"—and sometimes not too vaguely–"remember living in the Pleiades. I remember flying at the speed of light. I remember great spaceships activated by my energy, activated by thought. I remember..." And then you put it in the future, as a story, saying, "Well, this is a time to come." And yet you would not have that "story" within the consciousness right now if it were not something that you have already experienced.

All of time is as a sphere, and every point of time-related experience is within that sphere. Every point of experience which you would call "in the past" is within that sphere. Every point of experience which you would call your future is within that sphere. As you will contemplate another point of experience from where you see yourself now to be, what connects you is the line, and that is why you believe in linear time; yet it is a sphere of experience within a concept called time. Not every dimension of reality is constrained by the concept of time.

In fact, you are moving yourselves out of that sphere, that bubble of time. You even have the saying, "I am running out of time," or, "I am out of time." You are bursting the bubble of the concept of time and going beyond it.

Play with the revelations as they come to you. Allow them to fall into place, into a new understanding, a new gestalt, and see where that will take you. Then allow yourself to breathe and just be. Allow yourself, when you have followed the revelations as far as they will take you, just to be.

Know yourself to be the expansion of Allness. Know that you experience realities and you express as energy, as you understand that upon this plane. Also know that you express as the consciousness of Isness in other realities and dimensions, and what allows the expression and the experience of all of the dimensions and the realities is the interdimensional You, the matrix of You which is not confined to any specific point of reality. That is the ocean of Isness.

I have likened it unto love, and I have spoken with you in what you call olden times to be in the awareness of love, to know yourself as love, for as you will claim the beingness of love, you know expanded understanding of Allness.

Love is expansive. Even what you know as human love is expansive. When you have been caught up in love with someone your whole world changes. You feel yourself to be greater than what you have ever known yourself to be. You feel the object of your love to be even greater than what you have ever known anyone to be, and the experience goes beyond anything you have known the world to be. You would do anything to stay in love. It is rejuvenating. It is a wonderful place to be, and human love is but a sampling of the Love which is truly you, the Isness of You. I have characterized the Isness of You by explaining it as love, and yet it is much more than human love.

All of you are beloved of the Father. You struggle through your days. You have goals, activities which must be accomplished in every day. You have to go here. You have to go there. You have to be a certain persona. You hope you will measure up to what the employer wants you to be. You hope you will measure up to what the mate wants you to be. You hope you will measure up to what the friends, the peers expect you to be. You hope, in the deepest recesses of you, that you will measure up to what you think you might be. That is the toughest one of all.

And all the time you are beloved of the Father, wondrous, wondrous being which is you. You play a game. You play an all-star game and you are the star. You get into a most specific focus, knowing that you must connect with the ball which is coming towards you, and you must play according to the rules—arbitrary rules—of the game, and you hope that you can measure up. When you do connect, you feel so alive and all the time you are playing the game, the Self of you is sitting in the stands, if you will, watching the you which is playing the all-star game, cheering you on.

The matrix of You, the interdimensional You, is the source of your power of expression and experience. It is out of the matrix, the interdimensional You, that you manifest every reality which you experience. Out of the matrix of You, you fashion every experience within every reality. You do it so wondrously in this reality that you do not even know you are doing it.

If you would see something in your life experience transformed, expand into the interdimensional You, the matrix of You, the Isness of You, the Love of You. Allow yourself the deep breath which we have spoken of so often.

For when you take a deep breath, it opens the door to the Allness of You. It opens the door to the matrix of You, and it gives you opportunity to connect in remembrance once again with the creative power which you are.

Take the deep breath. If there is anything in your life experience that you would see transformed, breathe. Allow, with that breath, the inspiration of the Spirit of You, the interdimensional You, the Isness of You. Allow that space of change.

For when you will be focusing most specifically upon whatever is occurring in your life and you have the nose pressed right against the problem, how much of it can you see? Not much. You are right into it. But as you will allow yourself the deep breath and you can stand back a bit, you allow the connection once again with the Allness of You, the creative Allness of You. And in that instant of allowance and of connection, infinite wisdom—which is You—is available, ready and forthcoming, and there will be an idea which comes to you or a new perspective which says, "Perhaps I have seen this amiss. Perhaps that which I was calling a problem has been a gift. Perhaps that which I struggled against so hard has been the very process of awakening for me. Perhaps there is another way of looking at this."

You will see a miracle. It will transform whatever you have called a problem up to that point, for there will be wisdom, guidance, inspiration which comes from the interdimensional You which is not specifically tied to any experience or expression of a reality.

Now, the interdimensional You—ah, now we come to a most important point, a blasphemous point according to many—is the Father. It has been recorded in your Scriptures that I said, "I and the Father are One." And I am, and you are. The interdimensional You is the Father. You are not separate from the Father. You are life, are you not? Are you alive? Yes. You are expressing; you are creative, very creative: in every day you create drama for yourself, ideas, experiences.

The self of the present reality comes from the interdimensional You, which is the Father, the creative One. It is out of the interdimensional You that you create every reality.

Now, if the interdimensional You and the Father are One, and I assure you that you are, is there anything that you cannot transform? All power in heaven and on earth is given to you, quite literally. You manifest every reality. You call it good or bad or any gradation in between. Sometimes within a day's time you will go from interpreting an experience from one perspective to the opposite. You will have an experience with someone and you will feel, "I was certainly stupid. I didn't say the right thing; they didn't say the right thing," to the place where perhaps in that evening you will say, "Father, I see it differently now. I forgive even the previous judgment of myself and of that other one, for I didn't understand the whole vision. I only saw part of it." Within just the space of a day or even part of a day you have transformed a reality which you have experienced, because you have seen it differently.

If you and the Father are One—and I assure you that you are—if you are the interdimensional You having an experience, a human experience—and that is what you are doing—is there anything to fear? In Truth, no. Take yourself lightly, for, does the Father fear? When you are in the space of great love, even human love, there is no room for fear, for judgment, for seeing anything less than perfection.

For example, say you have met the most wonderful person. He is the object of your fascination. He is most handsome, intelligent, kind, wise, caring, and understands every mood you have. He is the epitome of your dream man. Or, you have met this most wonderful, gorgeous woman. She is most attractive and, besides that, she understands you. She is intelligent, but not too intelligent to show you up. She is intuitive. She knows exactly what needs to be said to soothe the ego, to praise you, to bring out the best in you. She loves to play with you. She loves to go anywhere you want to go. She is satisfied with whatever you will offer her, a most wonderful being.

You are totally and completely in love with this one. You feel your heart wide open. You feel expansive. You feel loved by this one and, more than that, you feel yourself in the flow of Love with this one. You know this one to be incarnate Love.

Now, a brother looks upon the object of your love and he is coming from a different place. He sees this woman to be most devastating energy, most bitter, selfish, greedy, critical even to the place of wanting to do you in. A sister looks upon the object of your love and she sees one who will run roughshod over you and will trample you.

But where are you when you are in that space of great love? You are not in fear of this other one at all. Great love has no room for any fear. Great love is so expansive there is not room for fear or judgment.

The interdimensional You, the matrix, the wholeness of you is great Love, greater than human love. Out of this interdimensional You, the Isness, the expansive, infinite Being which is not even contained as a Being, comes every reality which you experience. Even a reality such as your present one which has a collective consciousness based in the belief of duality, of good and evil, opposites and threats, can be and will be transformed as you live from the space of the interdimensional You.

In other words, see yourself as the ocean rather than the ship upon the ocean. See yourself to be the ocean rather than just the drop of water. Know that you are having the experience of the drop of water as you choose to know individuality, but truly you are the Allness of the ocean and the expansiveness which goes beyond even the concept of ocean.

In times when you will push out the boundaries of this reality, in times when you bring to yourself great motivation to know who you are, in times of sorrow, times of fear, times of worry, times of "what if," allow yourself the deep breath. Allow yourself to connect with the expansiveness which the deep breath affords you and go into the interdimensional You.

Chapter 1

Go into that space of perfect peace, of love. Know yourself to be held lovingly always within the arms of the Father, of the Mother, nurtured, cared for beyond even human concept of nurturing, and then breathe from that space of total love and total trust.

If you find yourself nose to nose with a challenge, breathe and go within to the place of the interdimensional Isness of You, the place of great peace, the place which cannot be threatened by any of the world. Breathe and go within and claim the peace, and breathe and breathe and breathe and breathe until there is a transformation.

The eyes of the body may show you possible threat, but you, as the great creative One, have the power to choose. You built the aspect of choice into the belief system of this reality, and it is a wonderful thing, the power of choice. So when the eyes of the body will show you an appearance, when the eyes of the mind will show you an appearance which could be threatening or less than perfect, breathe and choose again. If you have to breathe until midnight and if you have to breathe until the next sabbath and if you have to breathe until the next year, continue to choose to breathe and claim the peace and the love which is in that space, momentary as it may seem to be. Breathe and choose anew.

If you get into a confrontation with someone and there is a certain feeling of great energy which rises up within you known as anger, you have even within this reality the tool known as counting to ten before you would speak. Counting to ten allows you a space for a breath, does it not? Hopefully, somewhere in that counting you will stop and have a breath, and it allows you the gift of choosing anew.

You have come seemingly as a pilgrim into a strange land, and yet you have brought with you most wonderful remembrances. The first thing that you do within this reality as you begin to activate the body is to breathe. It is a most wondrous gift. If you would transform anything which you see in your experience, breathe and then go with that sense of peace to the next revelation. It will not be denied you.

You can deny it for yourself, for you can choose in the next moment to be right into the fray and to give in to the appearance, but you can also choose to breathe again and to claim the revelation of peace.

If you keep on breathing long enough, that which has troubled you will take care of itself. It will disappear. I hear you say, "Well, Jeshua, there are some circumstances that don't seem to be quite that easy." I assure you that if you will breathe for the next five years of your timing, that which has seemed so big in this day will be a bit diminished.

The interdimensional You is the place out of which you draw all power to create. It is a place of deep peace. It is a place where you know that, "I and the Father are One. I Am. I Am from before time began, and always and forever I will be, even beyond the concept of time." The interdimensional You is the Christ of your being. It is the Christ light, as you have concept of light. That is the closest thing you know within this physical reality which speaks of expansiveness, and yet the Christ of you is all light, all love, and beyond that.

Ascend unto the height of knowing the interdimensional You. Ascend into the most creative, miraculous space which is You. Claim your divinity. Claim your Christhood and live as the Christ even within this reality. Play with ideas of the mind. That is what the mind is for. Play with those ideas. Be creative. See where they will take you. Do not be conformed to world belief, but see where those ideas will take you, and then breathe and go even further into the Isness of You.

This world is a playground which you have made. It is very much as a playground where you see the small children playing. Some of them run about quite freely and are most in awe of what the body can do: how they can run very fast; they can do the somersaults; they can climb the trees; they can fall from the heavens and bounce when they hit the earth.

Others come with fear, and they feel that if they fall they will get hurt, and they do. The world which you have made is a playground, and as you have known old baggage from other lifetimes, old beliefs, sometimes you have fallen and you have said, "Because of old belief, I must be hurt."

Know that there is an instant, before you claim what an experience is, where you have choice? Know that sometimes information may be given to you that a loved one has passed on. There has been an "accident" and they have deceased the body. In an instant when that news is being delivered to you there is a choice point, a point of choice where you have said, "This isn't true. Maybe this is true. I have choice about this."

For just an instant there has been a feeling of, "I can make choice about this." Then the world belief comes with all of the old baggage which you have known throughout many lifetimes and have accepted as real, and the old baggage says, "It must be true. There is sorrow; there is loss within this reality." But there has been a moment of choice where you have known for a fraction of an instant that you could either accept the news as real or not.

Now you are moving to the place where you are beginning to understand that the world is of your making and that it is a playground. Yes, there are times when you are going to fall down, and the habitual understanding is that you are going to get hurt. But you are also moving to the place where you have experienced falling down and you have said, "Well, miracle of miracles, I don't feel hurt. What happened?" I will tell you what happened. You moved into the space of the interdimensional You long enough to know that you could see it differently. In other words, you claimed a new perspective. It had all of the makings of a tragedy. It had all of the makings of something really negative, and yet you have not felt that it was bad at all. It is because you are moving into a new place of understanding the world. You are the creator of it, and no longer does the baggage of old belief have to be part of this reality.

You are allowing yourself a space, albeit small, but it is growing, a space of choice; a space which says, "I can see this differently. I don't have to be hurt. I don't have to feel loss. I don't have to be ready with an answer. Whatever they said/did, that was their thing to do. What is it to me?"

If you will ask yourself that question, "What is that to me?" in the moment before the reaction comes, and breathe, you will find that all wisdom and all power is yours. Many times there is no response that need be given except to smile. You know how a smile confounds another one who would find himself in constriction and in anger. A smile offers the other one choice, and sometimes they do not want to see choice because they are sure how the avenue has to go. As you smile at them, you give them a choice of either letting it go and smiling back or keeping on with all of their energy, which very soon will fizzle out anyway if you do not feed it. There is great power in a smile. You do not even have to put words to it.

Chapter 1

Call upon the Reality—capital "R"—of the interdimensional You, the matrix out of which you have this experience. Call upon the Isness of You as often as you can remember. As you will practice breathing and being in the space of great expansive love of self and others, you will find that it becomes easier and easier to abide in the place of the beholder, of watching the game, knowing that you are in the game—you are playing it—but you are also the beholder, and you are the one who can change even the rules of the game, and you can bring yourself Home.

Come Home, beloved one.

Moving Into Interdimensional Consciousness

In the last chapter we spoke about the interdimensional You. We spoke of how there is focus, a most wonderful focus, upon this reality and the individuality which you see yourself to be, a focus upon a certain dimension of reality. And we spoke about how you are also expressing and experiencing in other dimensions, all in what you would see as the same slice of time. We spoke also that you are experiencing and expressing in different dimensions which do not even know time, a reality of non-time, where the concept of past and present and future does not exist, for there is only the present Isness, only the Isness of Creator Being. We spoke about how you as the individuated energy which you see yourself to be has come forth out of Allness, the interdimensionality of You, the Isness which is not focused upon any dimension or any reality—small "r". We spoke about how wonderful you are as an extension of all that the Father/Mother/One Source is, and how you draw the power to experience any dimension from the place of the interdimensional You. That is truly where you live: in the space between dimensions.

You believe yourself to be having a dimensional experience; you are within a certain reality—small "r"—and you have scripted that there will be certain parameters to the dimension. You have scripted that there will be a collective consciousness, that there will be the concept of time, that there will be the concept of space, the concept of physicality, and that there will be certain agreed upon laws which govern the physicality.

Now, in Truth, you are beyond any physicality. In Truth, you are the one who is determining moment by moment what the physicality means and what all of the physical "laws" mean. You are the one in a collective mind who is agreeing moment by moment that there will be such a thing as gravity, and you agree that because of gravity there will be certain weight which will hold you upon the ground.

You have also decreed that you will sometimes know weightlessness, that you will know non-gravity, and you will decree what the rules and regulations are that govern non-gravity.

You have felt governed by the "laws" and rules to the point where you have said that you do not have power over these "laws," that you are but a pawn, a victim sometimes, governed by all of the laws of physicality. And yet, you are the ones collectively who have decreed what the parameters are going to be.

The present reality where you find yourself to be is a dimension of reality based upon a collective belief in duality. Everything has one side and the other side. There is good and there is non-good; there is light, there is dark. Everything has an opposite. This is a reality which is based upon the collective belief in duality, and yet what you are seeking to know is your wholeness, your oneness.

It is a most miraculous, wondrous thing which you do as a bridge person, for you know well how to be within this reality—it is not always comfortable, but you know well what the rules and laws are, even down to the "shoulds" and "shouldn'ts" of contemporary arbitrary society—but you also are not content to stay at that place. You read; you discuss; you think; you meditate; you allow yourself to daydream. You allow yourself to go beyond what has been the usual thinking and to go outside the box a bit.

Even as you have been reading this, you have been going in and out of this dimension of reality, for as I am speaking you focus upon what I am saying, but there is also an idea that comes and you go off for a nanosecond onto a new idea.

You go in and out, even though it seems to be a continuum of focusing upon this reality. You will think about the ideas, the concepts that we are speaking of, and there is a glimpse of expanded reality, even though you would say that you are attending to the message in a continuous fashion.

As we are speaking of the interdimensional consciousness there is a focusing which you do upon this reality, this time, this here and now, but there is also a part of you which is the beholder. Have you experienced the beholder? Have you felt yourself at times to be just somewhat removed from what was going on? You felt yourself to be in conversation with someone and yet there was a part of you which stood about shoulder-side and was watching everything that was happening?

When you are in the space of the beholder, you are allowing yourself to expand the consciousness into the interdimensional You. Now, the beholder is not the interdimensional You, but it is a step in the process of knowing the interdimensional Isness.

When you are taken over by a sense of peace which does not make sense to the world, that is the beholder of you, the expanded Self of you beckoning to you to stay in that place of peace and allow all of the rest of the activity to be whatever it needs to be.

You have experienced the interdimensional consciousness, and yet it has been your agreement so far that you would focus upon this reality and this dimension. Your agreement has been by divine agreement for a divine purpose. It has not been a mistake. It has been to fulfill a divine purpose: to know intimately this dimension and this reality and to know completion with it.

You and the brothers and sisters, collectively, with whom you now share this reality have agreed that you would focus most intimately upon a certain reality to the place where you would know how it feels to experience all the parameters of the reality. "I know how it feels to be happy; I know how it feels to be sad; I know how it feels to be on the mountaintop; I know how it feels to be in the pits; I know how it feels to love and be loved; I know how it feels to be, as I perceive it, on the outside of love; and I am complete with the belief in duality."

You have decreed that you would focus most intimately upon this reality, and yet all the while the still small Voice has been whispering, "Remember, this too shall pass. Remember, you are more than what you have believed yourself to be. Remember and hope." Have you heard the still small Voice of hope? Of course you have.

You have agreed that you will know this dimension and know it intimately. You will know all of the laws of physicality. You will know how it feels to activate a coalescence of light energy known as a body. You will know how it feels to activate various forms of body—not only the human body, but all forms of life—and you will come to the place of knowing your oneness with all of life and all of its forms. For indeed, you have been every form of life which you can imagine or think of, and it is time now that you begin to cultivate the remembrance and awareness once again of oneness with all of Life.

In your process of awakening, which is happening now, it is time and it is imperative that you practice expanding the consciousness beyond just the individuality you have seen yourself to be. You are the one who has agreed to be the bridge person; you are the one who is remembering now that you have agreed to be the light even in the darkness of forgetfulness which is yet upon this plane, this reality. In your agreement, you have said that there will be a time when you will expand the consciousness beyond the individuality. That time is now. That is why you feel such a driving motivation within yourself to read, to study, to discuss, to contemplate, to seek, to want to know more. You have said, "In the process of awakening, there will come a time when I will know that I am much more than the body, much more than the personality I have seen myself to be, much more than the personality I keep working on to make better, much more than the individuality that I know is most wonderful and yet I can't quite always be happy with it. There will come a time"—and this is now–"when I will begin to expand my consciousness to know the interdimensionality, the Reality of me. I will come to know and to touch that space, the matrix, the Isness of me, the extension of the Father."

When you come to the full realization that the matrix of you, the interdimensionality of You which is not focused upon a dimension or a reality, when you come to the realization that, "I and the Father are One; I am an extension of the Father," when you come to realize that the matrix out of which you function and fashion everything which you experience is of the Isness of the Father, you become transformed. No longer can you look at the happenings in your world, in your life, in the same way. For truly, you begin to look upon all of the activities of the world, all of your experiences, through the eyes of the Father.

Then there is a sense of having come Home to the realization that, "I am so loved of my Father that never have I left Him, never has He left me. In Truth, I cannot, for I am an extension of the Father. I, in the interdimensionality of me, know my oneness with the Father. I am the Christ."

Now, how do you begin to expand the consciousness into the interdimensionality of you? You breathe. You allow the expansion of the body, mind, and soul which comes with a single deep breath. If ever you are in a constricted place of worry, breathe. Remind yourself, discipline yourself, do it. It takes a bit of discipline because you have to choose. Now, you know that when you breathe you are going to have opportunity for peace, and you do not always want to choose for peace. Let's be honest here. Sometimes you want to abide in the drama for awhile.

But when you choose to breathe, then you have opportunity to know a moment of peace, a moment of expansion. Breathe now. Take a deep breath. Drink deeply of a deep breath and feel the peace of you which comes with the breath. Then breathe again.

Even though there may be many cares and concerns, decisions that have to be made, allow them to be put aside for the moment of a breath, and breathe again. Feel the expansion which happens even within the body. Feel the very cells themselves expand and speak back to you in gratitude, for you are allowing them to breathe, allowing them to be at peace within themselves.

All of the troubles of the world will be there waiting for you whenever you choose to go back and pick them up. But if you choose to abide in the peace of the breath, they have no power over you. They will wait until you attend to them, and if you choose not to attend to them, they will have to keep on waiting, and you may breathe and breathe to the place of just being, to the place of deep, deep peace; a healing peace. If the body is giving you a message of constriction known as disease, you can breathe it into health. Throw a little joy in as well.

For indeed, as you breathe and you allow yourself to abide in peace, after awhile there will come an idea, a humorous idea. It just comes and tickles the soul. It is a place where you feel a little bit of joy bubbling up, and it will heal the body if you will allow yourself to stay in that space.

Meditation

Allow yourself now to take another deep breath, and allow the body to feel easy; allow the eyes to relax, allow them to be very soft. Take another deep breath and feel the peace which comes in with that breath, and feel yourself as light. Know that the light of you surrounds the body, activating the body. Feel the light all around you, a very easy, golden white light which illuminates everything; a very soft, gentle light.

Breathe again, and in that space begin to allow the receptors of the mind to extend, to reach out to a loved one, one you have known, one perhaps who is not activating the body any longer, or one who is activating the body. Allow the mind to expand, to reach out to that one, to be in communion without words, just in love, in peace. Hold that one in the mind's eye gently, easily. Be with that one in light.

Then speak silently to that one whatever you would say to them. Speak silently to that one whatever your heart would say to their heart, the innermost being of you to their innermost being, and feel the oneness, the communion, the togetherness.

Now listen. What does that one say to you? Receive what that one will say to you.

Bless that one with your love. Bless that one for coming to your awareness, and know that any time you wish to speak with that one, there are no barriers to communion, to communication.

Now allow the mind to expand, to reach out into what you would see as perhaps a distant time; to a master, a teacher, a guide perhaps; one who has been with you throughout many lifetimes; one with whom you would speak; one with whom you would converse. Even if you do not know what this one might look like, allow yourself to feel the presence of this one's intelligence, this one's being.

Embrace this one's presence with your awareness. Speak to this one; ask of this one whatever question you would be carrying.

Then listen.

You may feel the answer in words; you may feel the answer come in a picture, a vision. You may feel the answer in just a knowing.

Now bless this one for the friendship, for the communication, for the love, and know again that any time you would speak with this one, they are there at your invitation—any time, any place—for truly there is no separation.

Again take a deep breath of spirit and allow the mind to expand. Throw it open and invite whoever would speak with you to be in your presence and in your awareness. Welcome them. Ask of them who they are, why they have come, what message there would be for you. Breathe again and feel the expansion of the mind and heart in the place of oneness. Know that your mind expands far beyond this point of reality. Breathe and feel the deep, deep peace of the one Mind which knows no time or space.

Bless the one who has come to you, and know that any time you may pick up the strand of this communication again.

And now, taking a deep breath, allow yourself to feel the energy of you coming back to this point of focus. Be aware of the mind of you. Be aware of the body that you activate. Be aware of the room around you. Be aware of the peace which is you.

Know that you have touched the place of interdimensionality, the place which goes beyond the reality of this dimension.

When you allow yourself communication with ones whom you do not see with the physical eyes, you move beyond what has been understood to be the reality of this dimension. You expand the mind. You expand the possibility, the probability, and the reality you accept as the collective agreement. In other words, you have moved beyond the specific reality and you begin to know communication beyond this dimension.

What we have touched upon briefly you may expand. I suggest, I very strongly suggest, that you expand it in your times of quiet; that you set aside time in every day to breathe, to be at peace, to expand the mind, to speak with masters; that you be in communication with loved ones. Whether they have released the body or are activating a body in this reality does not matter, but be in communication with them beyond what you see as the body and the tones of the voice. Set aside some time in every day to be willing to be of assistance to whomever will come into your consciousness as you sit in that expanded state. Set yourself as a beacon of light, as it were, to help, to assist, to aid, to guide any consciousness, any being who may come seeking you in that place of light, setting aside all sense of small self.

Now we have taken the first step. Later we will take it beyond even what has been understood to be concept of being, concept of energy. For in this time we still spoke of concept of being where you would contact or receive contact of energy. In subsequent times we will speak of going beyond even concept of being into the place of Isness where there are no words, no concepts, only love. And we will come to understand that it is Love, and yet not love as the world defines it.

I suggest very strongly that you allow yourself ten minutes in every day to expand the mind into the peace of you. Be like the microphone which reaches out to find sound. If there is sound, the microphone focuses on that sound. If there is silence, the microphone reaches out; it must find sound somewhere.

Allow yourself to reach out with the expanded mind. Allow yourself to know the great peace and the healing which is yours for the claiming. Allow yourself to know the peace of being, just of being, for ten minutes and longer. I guarantee that when you try it for ten minutes, you are going to desire to abide there longer.

Know that you will find me in that place. Do not be surprised, for I inhabit that space all of the time. It is Home, and I stand ready, willing, able to welcome you Home in that space whenever you will choose to turn the focus of your attention wide open to feel the joy and the peace of your being.

Come visit Home, beloved one.

The Out-of-Body Experience

Beloved one, I would speak with you now about the out-of-body experience, for indeed there is within this reality much focus upon the body. It is what holds you in the specific focus of physicality.

For you know and you feel the body. You hear its messages, the creaks and groans, the twinges, the outright clamor at times. You feel yourself very much identified with and circumscribed by the body, and yet you will not come to the understanding and acknowledgment of the interdimensional Self unless you release the specific focus upon the body.

Now, I do not mean you have to decease the body, but I do mean that in your expanded understanding you will need to release the specific focus that says, "This is all there is to me."

You have read books and you have heard ones speak about the out-of-body experience, and it has seemed to be quite strange, miraculous, mystical, something very different from whatever you have experienced. You have felt, "Those who can have an out-of-body experience must be next to mastery; they must be close to being a guru; they must be close to being perfected expression. It is not something that I know how to do." Yet I will say to you, you have done it even in this day.

You have had out-of-body experiences even in this day, for there have been times in this day that the mind has wandered. You have gone into other realms. You have thought about a friend somewhere, not physically present with you. You have even thought about what you are going to do on the morrow. Where was your specific focus on the body in that moment? Gone.

In truth, you have been out of the body more than you have been with the body experience even in this day. So the out-of-body experience is not something that is beyond you. It is something mystical; it is something wonderful, for it speaks to your unlimitedness, but it is not something which is reserved only for those who have practiced and practiced and practiced and become pure of heart, as you would judge purity of heart. It is something quite natural.

The out-of-body experience is one of the steps in ascension. It is most necessary to know expanded experience beyond specific focus of physicality in order to know ascension.

The wonderful Truth of you is that you are not held to the body. You bring your focus of attention to the body from time to time; you activate it by the creative spirit which you are, but you are not dictated by the body as to what you do. Even the ones who would experience inflexibility of body are, in Truth, by the holy spirit of them, decreeing that they will express and experience a certain inflexibility of body. Those who would say by all appearances that they have no mobility of body, in Truth have the mobility of spirit which allows them the immobility of body.

You have wonderful examples of this in your day and time: brothers and sisters who have volunteered to be as visible examples for you. And they have known by their own experience that, in Truth, they are not the body. You have one who is most visible in this day and time who was well known as he activated the body with a good bit of mobility. He was one of your movie personages, a star, as you call them. Wonderful terminology, for this one is quite a light. This one was very visible as the movie star and then has come through an experience which the world would judge to be tragic. Yet he has found himself alive and well as the spirit which he is, carrying on a new role as spokesperson for all those who are experiencing immobility.

This one's choice of name even foretold his role in this day and time. This one, "Christopher" meaning Christ-bearer, Christopher Reeve, is showing to the world and to himself that the spirit is indomitable. The spirit is what activates the body, not the other way around, and he is finding himself, even though the body is temporarily immobilized—hear that well, temporarily—more alive now than previously.

So when occurrences happen in your world, look first with the eyes of the world—do not deny the language of the world—and acknowledge the appearance, then go beyond that to ask, "What is the gift in this? What is the whole truth in what seems to be limited?"

Everything you witness, every experience is as the pointer which points to Home if you will but have the eyes to see, to look a bit deeper, to open the blinders so that you have a whole view, the holy vision.

You are coming now into a most miraculous time where it is going to be asked of you that you move into the interdimensional Self in order to have understanding to deal with occurrences in your human life. Now, when I say this, it is not to put fear into you. It is not to speak of doom and gloom, for indeed you have written into the life script enough of the doom and gloom catalysts which are going to bring you to the most wondrous place of remembrance. You are going to see loved ones deceasing the body. Begin to practice communication now. Begin to practice now how it feels to go in this world with a focus upon the world, yes, but with an expanded focus of Self.

Begin to be the beholder of self—small "s". Begin to move into the sandals of the Self—capital "S"—and walk in those sandals at the same time you walk in the sandals of the self—small "s". You can do it. You will not lose sight of who you are. You do not have to worry that if you begin to expand into the understanding of the true Self of you that you are going to lose the thread of this reality. You will be able to find your way back easily.

Begin to work with knowing expanded Self. Be aware of the out-of-body experience in every day. Be aware that you are not the body. Be aware of the power of the holy Child to create, out of the interdimensional Self, the dimension which you call reality. Even when the reality—small "r"—is screaming at you, allow yourself to be the beholder, to be the Self—capital "S"—which stands back and applauds all of the drama that is going on around you. See how well you and the brothers and sisters play your part in the script, the collective script which you have agreed you will play. And then, every once in awhile for the fun of it, go into improv and change the script and watch how everybody has to scurry, asking, "What page are we on?"

Do a bit of improv every day. When you know what another one expects you to say, take a deep breath, and before you say the expected, come about it from another angle and see what happens. You will have a lot of fun with it.

You will also begin to understand the expanded Self of you and to understand how you are not held to what you have thought was reality. I am very much in favor of improv. It is what I did in my day and time when you walked with me, when the scribes and pharisees would ask me to interpret certain passages. I gave them some new meanings and a new way to look upon the writings, and they had to do a bit of scurrying within their mental computers to see how that could be, and most of the time they rejected it.

But the ones such as you, who were hungering and thirsting to remember, enjoyed the improv and you followed me. More and more of the brothers and sisters came to hear me, ones who wanted to know, "What new thing is he going to say today?" And I did not disappoint.

I was called radical because I enjoyed the improv. You will be called radical as you enjoy the improv and you throw in a new angle.

The out-of-body experience is a gift. It is the space where you move into the Reality—capital "R"—of you. It is a most wondrous space which proves to you, even while you have the focus upon a specific reality, that you are not held in that reality.

I see you do this as you are driving your vehicles. You are attending to the other vehicles on the road; you are attending to the little dial which says how fast you are going; you are attending to the steering of the vehicle, and then you begin to think, "I wonder who is going to be at the meeting? I wonder if they are going to serve any food? I wonder how late Jeshua is going to talk? I wonder what I'm going to do on the morrow? I wonder if the passage in the book that I was reading meant such and such?"

And then you come back to the body experience, and you look at the signpost and you say, "My goodness, twenty miles have gone by; where have I been?" You have been out of body. You have been in an expanded self.

As a child you have known the Allness of spirit. As a child I knew Allness of spirit. In the agreement that I made to know human experience and to know it intimately, there was a scripting where I would temporarily set aside the remembrance of Allness and would regain it by process and the belief in process, the same as you, and that I would manifest for myself at every turn the true and divine teacher, which I did, and which you are doing. And the teachers which I called forth were most wondrous, loving beings who served me as I serve you now.

What I impart to you now are the steps which were given to me as evidence of expanding thresholds. Step by step by step. For example, when you can, find an aromatic leaf, perhaps a leaf of mint. Breathe deeply of the scent of the aromatic leaf.

Crush it within the fingers so that you have the whole aroma of the aromatic leaf.

As you breathe the scent of the leaf, allow the eyes to go soft. Breathe deeply of the scent and go within. Go within the aroma. Feel yourself transported by the scent.

Allow yourself to breathe very deeply of the aroma and to know yourself at one with the scent. Breathe of it and go where it will take you. Breathe of it. What color is the scent? As it expands in your mind, allow it to take on a certain color. What color is the aroma? How expansive does it feel?

What does it bring as a visual to you? What memory does it hold?

Breathe deeply of it.

Now allow the consciousness to come back to this point of reality. Where was the focus of attention? Was it with green fields? Was it beyond the stars? Was it with a memory? Perhaps it was a feeling which does not have words.

It was a most mystical experience, an out-of-body experience, and yet using the most wonderful tool of one of the physical senses.

As I was a lad learning to release the focus on physicality, one of the other ways that my teacher taught me was to use the flame of a candle and to look at the flame with gentle eyes.

As you gaze upon the candle flame, allow the eyes to go soft. Keep this in the mind's eye and go within. Remember how the flame looks. Feel yourself within the flame, a cool flame, a beautiful color. Feel it expansive. Feel it to be you, expanding and expanding, dynamically alive. Be with it as long as you wish.

And now, breathing deeply, allow yourself to bring the consciousness back to this point of focus.

In those moments you released the attention upon the body and you traveled, if truth be known, into infinite space. You traveled into the magical place of creativity, for you were creating the journey as you went.

You may experiment with visualizing different colors, going within each color, expanding into the color, changing hues, etc. Allow yourself to be deeply within the color to see where it will take you. Some colors you may find more energizing. Some colors you may find more peaceful. Some colors may surprise you.

What the goal is here, is to go beyond what you have said this reality has to be. Allow yourself to play with the expansiveness of the creative holy Child. Allow yourself to move into the magical realm which does not know the boundary of reality. Another tool of physicality which allows you most wondrously to release the specific focus on physicality is the tone. If you have a windchime, a musical instrument, or a tone bar which will reverberate for a length of time, bring forth a tone, a lingering tone. You are again using a physical sense to transport you beyond the body. You know specific focus of physicality and then you allow that physicality to be as a doorway to experience your unlimitedness.

Feel yourself riding the wave of tone. Feel it within you. Feel it beyond you. Ride the wave of the tone and see where it takes you.

Do not be in a hurry. You may want to stay in that space a while.

Then, when you are complete, allow the consciousness to return to this point of reality.

Practice having the out-of-body experiences. Practice the expansiveness of the soul. Get in touch with the soul beyond this specific reality. Play with using the physicality to transport you beyond physicality. Play with the sense of aroma, the sense of the visual, the sense of sound, and go within to the inner senses and allow yourself to know the freedom of the holy Child. Touch the place of the interdimensional Self, the ocean of Being out of which you have fashioned this being. Go there often. Touch the place of peace. Touch the place of the Christ, for indeed that is where the Christ abides, and then walk this plane transformed.

For the times that you are calling forth now ask of you that you know how to be *in* the world and yet recognize that you are not *of* the world. *The world is of you.* The times now ask you to realize—to make real in your experience and expression—the interdimensional Self even as you go in a world which does not believe in the Reality—capital "R"—of you.

Bring Reality into realization. Live. Truly live. Bring the interdimensional Self into this life and come truly alive, for in that place you remember once again the Christ.

So be it.

Actualizing the Interdimensional Perspective

We have spoken of moving into interdimensional consciousness, being aware that you are carrying on the activities of living within this dimension—which is what you have agreed you will do—bringing your light to anchor upon this plane of reality. You will activate a body with your light quite literally, and you will also bring the light of your countenance, the light of your understanding, the light of your being to bear upon all of the issues of the world, so that you will be a light for the brothers and sisters who are seeking in the darkness to find their way Home.

Furthermore, you have agreed that by anchoring your light upon this plane you will come to know it for yourself. For indeed, that which you give unto others will not be held back from you, and in the giving you are blessed and receive as well.

We have spoken of moving into the interdimensional consciousness of allowing yourself to know that "I am *in* the world, but I am not *of* the world. The world truly is of me." Now you are able to bring a certain understanding to the specific focus of this reality, releasing the old restrictions of what has seemed to be reality to move into an expanded perspective.

We have spoken of various techniques for allowing the expanded consciousness to be within your awareness, and I spoke with you that I was leading you gently the way my teachers and masters had led me in my lifetime.

For indeed, I did not come unto the ascension without having done some practice. There were many years of study where I met with teachers and masters in my own country and abroad. I was fortunate—even as you are in this day—to be able to travel, to study with ones who have had revelation come forth from within them, and they were willing and ready to share it with me. You have, in this day and time, many of the brothers and sisters who offer the various gatherings where you can go and be touched by your revelations which have come through their remembrances.

Now I would speak with you about actualizing the interdimensional perspective; in other words, bringing it into actual experience, knowing that it can be real within your experience and real within this reality, and it will transport you beyond what you have seen as a limited reality, although wonderful even in that limitation.

First of all, I honor you for having come to a certain place of readiness, a certain place of willingness, of wanting to loose the bonds which have held you in constricted understanding. You have come to a place where, in truth, many of the old limited beliefs have begun to fall away, some of them gently; some of them have taken a bit more of the motivation, the challenges of life, to the place where you have had to stop to re-evaluate what is going on.

Whenever you come to a certain time in your lifetime where there is hindrance, where there is challenge, where there seem to be closed doors, count it all as blessing and rejoice. For indeed, that which you are bringing into your experience is the most divine motivation and catalyst for the expansion of your consciousness. It is as the seed which cannot grow unless it bursts its casing.

Before the casing of the seed is burst, there has to be much of energy brought forth. It is not done without a certain concentration of energy, divine energy. So when you will be facing the challenge which seems life-threatening, that seems to be threatening all that you hold dear, all that you have esteemed to be of value, call it all good and rejoice. For indeed, it may have backed you up against a wall and forced you to the place where you make new choice, new understanding. Even though you have been *willing* the previous moment to see things differently, in a certain moment of concentrated energy there will be the revelation which bursts the casing of what has been held to be reality and truth—small "t"—to a place where in the next moment you are as a transformed being. That is how powerful revelation can be and is.

You have known moments of revelation. A moment previous to the revelation you may have felt in the slough of despondence; you may have felt despairing that there could be an answer. You have sought high and low. You have prayed hard, have prayed gently, have called out to all of the masters, guides, teachers, and angels. You have gone down on bended knee to the place where you needed the knee pads after awhile, and you have prayed fervently, and yet you felt that there was some connection missing. In the next moment there was a blinding, transforming light, a revelation; or in the next moment there was such a gentle shifting of perception that you said, "Why didn't I see that before?" The shift in perception, the revelation, comes in many different ways.

But when it comes, you will no longer be the same as you were the previous moment and you go as a new—I will borrow a phrase which you have in your day and time—you will be a new person in Christ. You will be a new person in Christ, for you will begin to understand the Christ of you and the power of the Christ of you; not a new person in Christ as in saying, "I accept Jeshua the Christ as my savior who is going to work magic for me," but a new person in Christ because you begin to lay claim to the power of the Christ which you are, and that is all powerful beyond any dimension, beyond any reality. Then come forth the songs of joy.

For indeed, the Christ of you is as a child, the innocence of a child and the wisdom of a child, the child that has not been shaped and formed by the world, but the innocent holy Child of you. If you want to begin to know the Christ of you, look within to the child of you. Nurture that child. Speak with that child. At first there will be the certain encasement, the layering of the wounded child, the illusory layering of the wounded child.

Allow yourself to be nurturing to that child who says, "Yes, but I have tried. I have tried so hard." Be nurturing to that child, comforting, and say that "It is okay now, for I am beginning to understand the power of us"—the child and you as the consciousness you bring to it. When the wounded child brings to you various issues, various hurts, allow yourself to be with that child. Do not dismiss the layering which has happened. Do not dismiss the certain illusions, the certain untruths and say, "Oh, but that isn't true." Allow yourself to be with the wounded child in a place of expanded understanding and holy vision. Bring the holy vision to the wounded child and say, "Yes, I know that is what we have journeyed through, but here is the greater picture." Take the child by the hand, figuratively. Put your angel wings around that child of you and nurture that child with all of the love that you can feel and experience. You will feel a great wellspring of love coming from within you—more and more love than you have ever thought possible—and it will continue to grow. The angel wings which you put around that child you will see to grow in radiance and luminescence and in comfort.

If you want to begin to know the Christ of you, nurture the holy Child within you. At first you must approach it in the language that you know so well: the language of the world, the language of the wounded child . Do not try to leapfrog over to the place that says, "Oh no, you are the holy Child. Nothing has ever come to threaten you." Speak with the child of you in the language that is understood right here and now first, and then allow the love to transform all of the old wounds into the place of expanded understanding. You will begin to feel the Christ of you growing, the holy Child of you taking hold of your hand, saying, "Yes, I will come with you. Together we will grow as one."

You will come unto a certain place where there is not you and the child as seen as separate—as you communicating with the child and the child with you—but there will come to be known a oneness. The inner dialogue itself will change, and it changes through love.

It is not in this lifetime for you to deny the world experience. It is not for you to deny the body, to take yourself off unto the cave, the monastery, to say, "Well, that is the world. It is something bad. I will have nothing to do with it." This lifetime you have agreed that you will be a bridge, a conscious bridge from the interdimensional Self to the dimensional world.

Therefore, speak with the inner child with the language of the world, first of all, and then speak with it with the language of Truth, which is love, until you find it is speaking with you more powerfully and it is living you rather than you living it.

In Truth, the Christ Self of you is living this lifetime, but the creative you thinks that you as an individuality are doing it all. You have put up a certain barrier around yourself, and you have said, "This is me, and I am all alone in this, and I have to do it all myself, and maybe if I am good enough, if I pray hard enough, if I read the right books, if I listen to the right tapes, maybe I'll get a certain sense of not being alone."

In Truth, the Christ of you is living this life experience, and it is time now, as you have decreed, that you come to know the Christ Self which is living your life.

Now, how do you actualize this interdimensional perspective? How do you come from the perspective of Allness?

There are certain ways of actualizing the new perspective, which, in truth, is a very old, old perspective which goes back to the Reality—capital "R"—of you that is beyond and before time began.

I would invite you now to take a deep breath, and as you do so, feel yourself gentle. Breathe a deep breath easily in a circular fashion, breathing in easily without effort and out without effort.

In and out. In and out. At your own pace. Whatever feels comfortable. Feeling the peace which comes with the breathing. Feeling the healing which comes with the breathing.

Feel the expansion of self. Feel yourself no longer bound by the body. Yes, you have a body. You are activating it, but you are more than the body. Allow the breathing to be easy and expansive. Feel at peace.

In that state of peace, bring to mind easily, gently, an occurrence; something which has happened that you witnessed; an occurrence which happened between brothers, sisters, friends. Something which happened that you witnessed, that you saw. You were as a bystander. A conversation, perhaps, that you overheard or that you were privy to.

Allow it to play out in your mind's eye, what one said and how the other responded. You were just the beholder. Allow yourself to see not the bodies of each one, but to see the energy of the ones engaged in this encounter, in this dialogue. It may have been a dialogue of confrontation. It may have been a dialogue of friendship, of love. Allow yourself the perspective of seeing not the bodies now, but the energy, each one as a ball of energy, as light energy. Replay that encounter, that conversation, seeing the energy of the conversation, the encounter, the occurrence as it played out.

What is happening with that energy? Can you see it as dynamic? For indeed, the energy which activates the body and is carrying on a certain conversation is always dynamic, always changing.

Perhaps you will see it in certain colors. Perhaps you will just see it as light. Allow yourself a certain perspective as the beholder and watch how it plays.

And now, taking a deep breath, reflect on the occurrence which you just beheld, the replay of something that you witnessed and the truth of the energy which was happening in that encounter. The energy is a new perspective, is it not?

Now, I invite you to again take a deep breath and return to that sacred place of peace, back to the place of the beholder. Bring to mind an encounter in which you were a participant; something which happened perhaps in this day, in this week, where you were a participant engaged in a certain interrelationship with another brother, sister, or perhaps brothers and sisters, and review it in the mind's eye and let it play out. Review the occurrence. It may have been a time of confrontation where words were spoken. It may have been a time of possible confrontation where you would have liked to have spoken certain words but did not. It may have been a time of love, of support, of understanding; any of the above, but a time that happened when you were engaged and there were certain feelings that came to the forefront. Review that in the mind's eye. Who said what to whom? How was it said? How did you feel about it and what you said, or what would you have liked to have said?

Now allow yourself the perspective of seeing yourself as a participant, but not with the bodies. Again take the perspective of seeing the energy. What was their energy like as they were saying certain things? What was your energy like as you heard what they were saying? What was your energy like as you responded either verbally or silently? For indeed, you had a response. See the energy at play. Again, you may see it in colors or you may see it just as light.

Know that as it was occurring, the interdimensional Self, the Reality of you, was witnessing, watching what was going on, even though the focus of you was very much in the engagement of that occurrence. The interdimensional Self of you was perceiving the energy of the holy Child at play, the energy of the holy Child in expression and then internalized as experience.

Now, while you are still in that state of the beholder, that state of expanded perspective, allow yourself to say to that other one what your heart now says. What would you say to that one?

Allow yourself to see the energy that is at work now as you allow your heart to speak. Again, you may see it in colors or you may see it just as light. How does it feel? Know that you as the individuality are expressing and you as the interdimensional Self are beholding all at the same time.

If there has been an occurrence in your life that you wish you could go back to and change, an occurrence in your lifetime where you wish you could go back and say something differently or do something differently, allow yourself now as the interdimensional Self to bring the remembrance of that time to your awareness. Bring it into your awareness now and speak that which you would want to speak. Do that which you would want to do, and watch the energy.

For indeed, no moment of time is ever lost to you. You can call forth into the present moment any time which you feel has been or will be. In this space of the interdimensional perspective, in the space of the Reality of you, you can bring forth into your awareness any moment in time, and you can transform it. You can transform it now, and you can behold the interaction of the energy, and you can bring the blessing of the interdimensional Self to any event, situation, or occurrence. No moment of time is ever lost to you.

Now, taking another deep breath, bring yourself back to the present reality once again, feeling very peaceful, feeling healed.

Know that you can bring any situation, any occurrence into the conscious awareness of the now moment, and you can heal that which has seemed to be unholy and unhealed by allowing yourself to go into the holy space of the interdimensional You, the You which is not bound by this dimension, by this reality; the You which is truly the Christ you, the Christ Self. Do you see how freeing that is?

All of the old garbage which you have carried with you for lifetimes can be healed in the now moment, and you do not even have to sit and relive it. Much of the beginnings of the old garbage you do not even consciously remember, but you can heal it in the place of the now moment by going into the space of the perspective of the interdimensional holy Self and watching the energy.

Even if you do not know what the beginning of the unholiness was, the beginning of the wound which has seemed to be so deep, allow yourself a certain symbol of it and then watch as the energy of the now moment, the love of the now moment, engulfs it and transforms it.

No longer do you have to be held in the place of carrying old baggage of self and of others. No longer do you have to work through karma. No longer do you have to atone for sin as in the old understanding of atoning for sins. Yes, in Truth, you do have to atone: you have to come to that place of knowing oneness, at-one-ness with that which has been seen as the sin of separation. But you do not have to atone for old, old baggage in the usual traditional sense.

Allow yourself to come to the sacred holy space of the interdimensional You often. Bring it to mind at least once a day as you will lay the head upon the pillow. Allow yourself a moment before you drift off into the most wondrous sleep, a moment of being the beholder of all that has gone on in the day. See it as interaction of energy, and then bring the holy transformative light of love upon it as you would pour a certain oil, a balm upon anything which needed healing, and know that the day has been perfect, and know that you take that perfection into the sleep of the nighttime, and it will be there in the morning as a gift.

Now I would do with you one more powerful exercise—again, simple and powerful.

Allow yourself the deep breath, and with that deep breath feel yourself in the expanded state of the beholder. Allow yourself to breathe the expansion of the holy Self. Feel in the breathing a releasement of all that which has bound you to certain realities. Feel yourself expanding into the holy state of the beholder. Now look upon the body as you sit in the chair, as you recline, as you stand, and visualize the body in your mind's eye, the body which you call yours in this lifetime.

See it from the crown of you: the hair; what color is the hair? what style? is it long? is it short? is it dark? is it fair? is it curly? is it straight?

Allow yourself to see the forehead; the eyebrows; the nose, the nose which you often judge so harshly. Allow yourself to see your eyes; the radiance, the twinkling of the eye; the liveliness and the beauty of the eyes.

Look at the mouth and the chin. See the neck; the shoulders; the arms and the fingers. See the torso of the body and the legs down to the feet.

Look upon the most wondrous creation, the body which you call yours. It is a most wondrous creation. You have brought it forth in this lifetime, and you keep it activated by the Christ power that you are.

Now allow yourself to look upon the body as an energy field. Look upon the crown and see the light of the crown chakra. See the light which is radiant and glowing at the top of the head. Allow yourself to experience how dynamic it is, how changing it is.

Allow yourself to feel a pulsating, radiating energy field as the crown chakra. Perhaps you will see a color with it. Perhaps you will just see light. Either is okay.

Look upon the forehead, and see now the forehead infused in light. See it as radiant, pulsating. Look upon the throat and the throat chakra, and see it infused in light; see that light blending with the light of the forehead, no longer seeing the features of the face, but seeing only light.

The same for the torso: the heart chakra, the solar plexus. See the light of the body, very light, active, pulsating; no longer seeing the features of the body, but see light. See the light of the chakras at the knees and at the ankles; no longer seeing a certain form; seeing just light. Behold how the light dances, how it pulsates.

Allow yourself to think now of an occurrence, an interrelationship which you have had with one that was perhaps not too happy. Allow yourself to, perhaps, bring to mind a worry, a challenge, and watch the light of the body. See what happens to the light of your body. See what happens to the light, and see where and how it changes.

Now allow yourself to call to mind the time when you have felt most loved and loving; when you felt enfolded in the Father's arms and you felt you could do no wrong. You were the most blessed holy Child, the beautiful one of the Father; the beautiful one of a relationship, when you felt that the other one in the relationship was the most holy, beautiful one, and your heart goes out to them and engulfs them in your love. Watch the light of your body. See what happens with the light when you feel in that sea of love. See how it pulsates, how it radiates.

Know that you are so loved that, in Truth, you are the most wondrous creation of our Father. Know that you are His beautiful, perfect Child. Feel the perfection of the child which is you–innocent, holy, and wholly loved.

Watch the energy of the body which is you, and see that energy even as it sits upon the chair. See how it expands, how it radiates throughout the whole room, how it engulfs the whole room, the whole dwelling place; how it extends even beyond the confines of what you see as the atmosphere of this planet. See how powerful, how unlimited the light of the holy Child is.

Feel yourself transformed in that light, forever free, forever healed.

And now, breathing in the love of that holy expansive Christ which you are, feel the peace. Know that is holy space.

It is the Christ Child, and it is you. It heals you as the body. It heals you as the emotional individuality. It heals you as the soul.

For indeed, from this moment on, no longer are you the same as you were when you came to this message. You are transformed.

Now you will do a most wondrous miracle. With the eyes open, go within to the mind's eye and look upon the ball of light which is you that sits upon the chair, and bring to mind the most wonderful time when you felt so happy, so radiantly loved; so, so happy. And from ten feet above the body see that ball of light which sits upon the chair, and watch how expansive it is.

Even with the eyes open you are not focusing upon the outer, but you are focusing upon the inner. And that, beloved one, is actualizing the interdimensional perspective, no matter where you may find yourself to be.

In other words, you can be standing on a busy street corner with the eyes open, walking, attending to whatever needs to be attended to, and yet you can go within to the sacred place of the Reality of you and you can be the beholder all at the same time: that is actualizing the interdimensional perspective. That is living from the Christ perspective.

In truth, you know this perspective well. It is just that sometimes you have chosen to be so caught up in a specific reality, a dimension, that you have forgotten the interdimensionality of you which allows the dimensionality to be experienced.

If you will practice what we have done in these exercises, it will move you into a most wondrous place, a holy place which

will transform your life from here on, and it will, in Truth, bring you to the ascension.

Go now in peace. Go now in love, and remember Who you are.

So be it.

The Beholder

Beloved one, as we have been speaking of the interdimensionality of you, we have been speaking of the Reality of you, the Reality of the Mind of God. Now, "the Mind of God" sounds like a great phrase coined by some of your religious theologians. In Truth, the Mind of God is that infinite sea of Isness of which we have been speaking, and you are the Mind of God expressing in this point of focus as individuated energy.

You call yourself by a certain name. You know certain parameters of what you say your reality is. You have certain parameters of personality with which you identify, and yet, even as individuated energy, you are much more than the speck of consciousness. You are the Mind of God.

In previous messages I have been leading you gently, as my teachers and masters did, to the place of being the beholder, to the place of knowing interdimensionality. I would speak with you now in greater detail about the role of the beholder and how it allows you freedom from what you have seen this scripted reality to be.

Now, in this plane of reality which is based so much upon the belief in duality, you have made for yourselves a most wonderful dichotomy. On the one hand, you identify most specifically with who you say you are—the individuated energy—and you identify most specifically, most wondrously, with the experiences of this lifetime and of this world. You identify quite specifically with your creations, tangible and intangible.

On the other hand, you cry out to the higher Self of you or to me or to your Father God or to the Mother God to release you from that very specific identification. For indeed, as you will know constriction in that specificity, you want to know holy vision and you want to have your release from all that is binding within this reality.

So on the one hand, as you will be most wondrously identified with all of your creations, reveling in the drama of the adventure of the holy Child, at the same time within this reality that believes so much in duality there is a part of you which knows that you are not constrained to this reality and desires most wondrously to come up higher to know ascension out of this reality.

You have agreed that you will bring your light and anchor it upon this plane. You have agreed that you will play a certain role within the drama of this world; that you will walk with a cloak of forgetfulness where you will appear to be the same as the brothers and sisters, where you can speak a language that they understand; and yet you will commune with the greater Self of you to know that you are not constrained to this world.

The role of the beholder allows you the releasing of specific focus. It allows you to move into the extended consciousness of the greater Mind. It allows you to connect once again in the place of deep, deep peace with the Reality, the true Reality of you.

As you will allow yourself the simplicity of the deep breath, you have the opportunity to be at peace in that moment. As you will continue to breathe deeply and peacefully, you allow space for the still small Voice to speak, space for the inner wisdom which comes from the greater Self of you, the Mind of God. As you will assume the role of beholder, you find that it is not necessary—even as the world will speak to you that it *is* most necessary—to respond quickly to a brother's or sister's remarks.

You have taught yourself, because of the belief that you had to defend yourself and your creations, that it was necessary to have a very quick answer to ward off perhaps whatever would be coming. It was necessary to be seen as wise, all-knowing, for indeed, you did not want to be seen as a slow-witted one, for the slow-witted ones often were left behind, and you did not want to be left behind. Therefore, you have trained yourself to be very quick with an answer. It did not matter if you had thought it through or not, but it was important that you had an answer.

Now I am suggesting to you that it is important that you be as the wise one who allows yourself to play the role of the beholder, to breathe and to listen, and then to respond as the inner wisdom will guide you.

For indeed, you have known lifetimes when you have been the teacher, the master who had the various disciples and students around you, and there would be a question asked of you as the teacher, the master, and because you wanted to give forth truth, because you knew it was important that you be as catalyst for the students' own remembrance of their inner wisdom, you took your time in answering. Perhaps for a day, perhaps for a week you would sit in silence contemplating what the answer would be, and the students, because they revered your wisdom, waited; quite different from this day and time.

The students waited because sometimes the answer was not to be spoken, but to be revealed. The master, which you have been, knew that it was important for the mantle of silence to descend upon the group for ones to abide within their own being to find the answer to the question which had been asked.

In other words, it was important for them to learn the role of the beholder and just to watch: to watch the thoughts which would arise; to watch all of the possible answers which would come to the questions; to watch, to wait, to breathe.

There is great power in being the beholder and allowing yourself to come from the place of deep, deep peace and inner wisdom.

As you will get so caught up in all of the affairs of the world, what happens to the feeling of energy in the body? Know you that feeling? You feel like you are being pulled in many, many directions. You feel that you do not have enough energy to do whatever is being asked of you, and sometimes if it gets conflicting enough you have thrown up your hands and you have said, "I give up. I don't know what to do. I am supposed to be here. I am supposed to be there. I am supposed to know this answer. I am supposed to have this report done. I give up."

Great place to be, for indeed, in that moment you are releasing yourself from the demands of the world, even though the ego will not give you any accolades at that point. In that moment you are releasing all of the chains that the world has said it has around you, and you are moving into a place of surrender, a place which says, "I've done my best. I don't know what else to do now. Now I am going to stop. Now I am going to breathe." Blessed be the person who finds himself in that place and remembers to breathe. Then you have opportunity to move into the place of great power, the place of beholding, the place within where you ask for holy vision.

Now, the ego will be screaming at you that you have failed. The ego will be saying that you "should" be doing x, y, and z. But for a moment or so, bracket the voice of ego and say, "All right, I will tend to you in a moment or so. Get thee behind me for a moment. I am going to abide and behold for a moment. I am going to watch myself as I have been caught up in all of this constriction. I am going to watch the other ones who are also doing this dance with me. I am going to watch; I am going to breathe; I am going to ask for holy vision. I will know the power of silence, the power of the beholder."

There is great power in silence, for it allows you to connect once again with the Mind of God, the extended Consciousness. For indeed, the Mind of God is not a void. It is not a place of nothingness. The Mind of God is Allness. It is consciousness. It is awareness of the infinite. It goes beyond what the mind in this reality can comprehend. The power of the beholder is in the silence.

As you will assume the role of beholder, as long as you can remember—and it is a bit of a discipline—you will find great power in just being; great power in just loving, allowing: allowing the breath, allowing the holy vision, allowing the love and understanding to flow in to envelop you and all others who are in the most wonderful, divine dance with you.

Now I would invite you to take a deep breath. Feel the peace that comes with the deep breath. Take another deep breath and gently allow the eyes to soften, to turn the focus inward, to go within to the place of silence. Again I would guide you into the place of interdimensionality, the place of the beholder. We have done this before.

Feel the peace and the power of the silence. And in that space of beholding, call to the mind's eye an occurrence that happened in this day where you were witness to something which was going on between a brother and a sister, perhaps a group of people. Just allow yourself to think about what happened. Who said what? What did the body language look like?

In the place of the beholder, allow yourself to visualize the ones engaged in this encounter. Visualize them as a ball of light. Instead of seeing the features, the appearance of the body, allow yourself to visualize them as a ball of light, radiant, dynamic light. Replay again the situation and see how the balls of light interact with each other: which one seems more dynamic, which one is more aggressive, which one is more confused, constricted?

And in that space of the beholder, just watching the interplay of light, allow yourself now in a remembrance to balance the balls of light and see what happens. In other words, bring your healing consciousness, your holy consciousness to that event, and see each sphere of light being equal, radiant.

Then take another deep breath and allow that slate to clear, and call to mind an event, a circumstance, a situation in which you were a participant, an event where you were engaged with another one in the interplay of energy.

Remember the features of the other one as you were talking with them, conversing with them. How did they look? What did the face look like? What was the body posture? Then see yourself. How did your face look? How was your body posture? How did it feel? What was said? What was exchanged?

Then again, using the power of the beholder, allow yourself to visualize the other one and you as spheres of light, spheres of light activating the bodies. But now the appearances of the bodies, the physical boundaries of the bodies dissolve into light. See yourself in this interplay as light. Feel the interaction. How does your energy interact? Is it expansive? Is it contracting? How is their energy of light? Is it expansive? Is it contractive? Is it an exchange? Is it a blending, a mellowing?

Be aware of the nuances of the energy level of the spheres of light, how they dance. The light which activates the body is most dynamic and radiant. It is most alive. It expands, and sometimes it feels so expansive you could take in the whole world in your light. Other times you feel yourself to be a very small flame of the candle, surrounded by much darkness. Watch the interplay with the spheres of light.

Be aware of the subtlety of how the energy feels. Perhaps there has been something said to you which you did not want to hear, you did not want to believe. Perhaps something was said to you that you *did* want to believe. It was the most wonderful news you could have hoped for. How does that feel?

Using the power of the beholder, allow yourself to balance all of the spheres of light which have been within the mind's eye as you have replayed the situation. See all of the light blending, equal, dynamic, powerful, and loving. See the situation in a different light.

And now allow yourself to know that, in Truth, you have healed that situation. You have healed yourself. There is great power in the space of the beholder. There is great power in the space of the interdimensional You which is not caught up in specific focus and specific reality.

Whenever you want to know holy vision, allow yourself to move into the space where you have just been. Instead of seeing specific bodies, specific personalities, see spheres of light and see the interplay of light. It will release you from constriction of worry and fear and the "what if." It will release you from the voice of ego that says, "You should know; you should answer; you should be; you should have done, etc."—all of the "shoulds" the ego loves to offer you. The space of the beholder allows you to connect with the true meaning of you.

You have carried, throughout many lifetimes, much of armoring. You have carried it in the body. You have asked the body to be your perfect servant and to carry all of the beliefs of what you have said this reality is and has to be.

You come in this time, this day, with constriction, unease in the body. Some of you have allowed the unease to grow to the place of the threshold of disease. The body calls out to you and says, "I hurt. I need some loving attention."

It is possible to use the same technique that we just did to look at your body and/or to look at another's body and see where the constriction and armoring is. Now, in truth, you have lived lifetimes as the healer. You have lived lifetimes in which, because of a sincerity of heart, you desired to be of service to the brothers and sisters: to comfort them, to facilitate for them an ease of living instead of disease and suffering. You did not want to have the brothers and sisters in such pain and sorrow.

It is the same for you in this lifetime. Your tender heart cannot bear to see another one suffer. You have known how to see, to read one's body, through various techniques, to see where there is constriction. You have known to look even further than the body to see the wounds of that one's soul, wounds which have been carried throughout lifetime after lifetime and remanifest lifetime after lifetime because it was thought to be reality.

I invite you now, again, to take another deep breath—not with effort but just easy—and to go to the place within, the place of sacred silence, the place of peace.

Abiding in silence, bring to the mind's eye your own body as it would be in a mirror. You know what your body looks like in the mirror. Visualize the top of the head, the facial features, the throat, the shoulders, the chest area, the solar plexus, the thighs, the lower extremities of the legs, the feet, the toes. What do the toes look like? Visualize your arms, the top of your arms where they join to the shoulders, and the lower part from the elbow down to the wrists. Visualize your hands. What does the back of the hand look like? What does the palm of the hand look like? What do the fingers look like?

Now stand behind yourself and look at the back of the head. What is the shape of your head? What is the shape of the neck? How does your back look? your waist? the back of the legs? the back of the knees? the ankles?

Now, looking at the front of the body once again, allow all of those features, the boundary of the physical body, to dissolve into a very soft light. And scan from the top of the head down over the face, the throat, the shoulders, the heart, the chest area, the solar plexus, the legs and the feet, the arms and the hands. Is there a part of the body which stands out as more rigid? Is there part of the body which seems a bit darker than the rest? Is there a part which seems lighter than the rest?

And now stand behind your body and, again, seeing the light enveloping all of the body, scan from the top of the head to the heels. How does the light from the crown, the light from the back of the neck, across the shoulder blades, the chest, the waist, the hips, the back of the legs down to the feet, appear? How are the joints of the arms and the hands? the joints of the legs and the ankles?

Now, assuming the position of power of the beholder, allow your light to shine upon all of the body, especially any areas that seem to be a bit dimmer. Be as a great flashlight. Shine your light upon all of the body; wash the body with light from the back view, and then go around to the front of the body and wash the front of the body from the crown chakra down to the toes with light.

Be a cosmic flashlight; beam your light; wash the body in light. Claim for yourself healing in every cell of your body.

And then, abiding in the place of the beholder, in the place of silence, listen. Listen to what the body will tell you. If there is a part of the body that has a message for you, listen. Be as a friend to the body.

Place your light hands upon any part of the body that is speaking to you and receive the message. Reassure that part of the body that you are listening, that you have heard, that you care, that you will do all in your power to allow the light to flow into any constrictiveness in that part and throughout all parts of your body.

Breathe your peace into any part of the body that does not feel at ease. Expand. Allow your peace to expand the light of the body. Any part of the body which is registering constriction, allow the peace to expand every cell in that area and to shine the flashlight of your light into that area. See that area expanding. Feel it expanding. Know it is expanding. Claim it to be expanding.

Visualize turning your light on around the body. How does it feel? expansive? loving? healing? nurturing? You are calling forth the power of the Mind of God as you allow yourself to move into the expanded state of the beholder.

You are healing situations, experiences, perceptions, and even physical manifestation. If you will know ascension—and it is your desire to know ascension out of the constriction of the world and the reality that the world has dictated—practice being the beholder. Practice releasing specific focus. Practice knowing the light which heals all illusions.

This is what my masters taught me. This is what I give to you. It will heal everything you have experienced in this reality, and it will bring you to the place of great peace and Truth. It will bring you to the realization of the interdimensional You, the Reality which you are that is not focused upon or identified with anything dimensional.

In Reality you do not have specific focus upon any dimension. You are in the Reality of interdimensionality. You are in the Mind of God. Practice being that which you are. Practice being the interdimensional Truth. Practice being the beholder. The reward will take you out of this world.

When I speak to you of being the beholder, I speak to you of Truth, of steps which were given to me in what you call ancient times. When I speak to you of the power of the beholder, I give to you a key which releases you from specific focus. It does not mean that you will deny the world and the activities of the world; it means that you will know yourself to be *in* the world but not *of* it; that, in truth, the world is of your making.

Practice being the beholder and claim the joy which comes with knowing true freedom. And indeed, in that space of true freedom I am with you.

So be it.

Realities

Now, beloved one, I have a fun suggestion, something for you to do in the days ahead. I suggest you play with, "What can I imagine other realities to be? Perhaps a reality where there would be no time. How would that feel? Would it feel boring? Or would I put into it other aspects, creative aspects?"

Even as the question is asked, you know the answer, for indeed, you do live and experience and express within dimensions which do not know time, and yet you are not bored. You find much to do, to express, to be experienced in other dimensions even unlike this one.

You have made for yourself within this reality—and I speak of you as an individual and also as collective—quite a reality of challenge, a reality based on a belief in duality: good and evil, love and hate, and every subtlety in between. You even make for yourself the weather that can be a bit challenging, and you say, "Well, it is outside of me." But there is nothing outside of you. It is within your awareness, your consciousness and, in truth, you do create the weather patterns: you individually and collectively.

This reality which you call home—small "h"—is one of the more demanding realities. Think upon that. Is it a schoolroom? It has been likened unto a schoolroom. You can look at it that way. But in Truth, it is more; it is an adventure of the Creative. It is a most wonderful reality, in that it is as a catalyst to allow you to know the expanded Self and the creativity of the expanded Self, and all of the possibilities, even probabilities which you develop out of the possibilities into new realities.

It is a wonderful reality as a catalyst, for when you grow tired of the challenges—and it may take you eons of time; in fact, it has—you will ask, as you are asking now, "What more is there? There must be something more like heaven, more harmonious, where I can feel and know Home once again." With that thought you open up portals and you move into new realities even while maintaining this reality.

You have experienced even in this day going into new dimensions: going backward in what you call time, going forward in time, going into new dimensions of your imagination; and the question is asked, "Is it real?" It is as real as this dimension—real with a small "r"—coming out of the Reality—capital "R"—of the creative holy Child.

The new exciting time you are moving into has a new energy infusing this reality. You have felt it; a time when you are getting in tune with the creative energy of you, individually and collectively. This is why many are feeling a movement toward change. Some of you have moved to a new dwelling place. Others have the feeling, "I know I am going to move sometime, somewhere. I don't know exactly where it's going to be, but I know that it is going to happen. I know that there are changes coming about."

It is because you are as the pregnant ones who, as you have decreed, are bringing forth new reality in a new time, and it is exciting. Part of you is waiting as you would expect the birth of the new infant, waiting to see, "What is this one going to be like?" Yet, at the same time, nurturing with your meditation, with your energy, with your visualization, your visioning, the newborn which has not yet quite made the appearance.

Live in that space of excitement and expectancy, for in Truth, it is the portal to the place of remembrance of the creative energy of you. If you feel that you go along as on a treadmill, keeping up with things, sometimes perhaps barely keeping up with things, not being exactly excited about life, choose you anew to become excited. Find a new interest: a big one; a small one, something to become excited about. Fall in love. It is a good way to become excited about life. Fall in love with another mate if you do not have one now; a friend, perhaps; a beloved pet; an interest; even with the idea of what you can bring forth in a new time. Fall in love, truly in Love. Allow the excitement of new love to carry you to the place of realizing the Christ energy. That is where you stand right now. I cannot emphasize it too much. You stand right now on the threshold of realizing the Christ energy. Know you how exciting that can be? Take hold of it. Live with it. Go for it. Make the changes.

Long enough have you existed. Long enough have you acquiesced to what you thought the voice of the world said you had to do. Long enough. Come alive now in the Christ energy, the *Christos*. It is your birthright, and it is time to claim it. Do not be afraid, timid. Claim it.

Every day find a new way to become excited about how you are. Every day. You have had challenges which have pushed you to the place of developing new perceptions. You have had challenges, challenges which have at the time seemed almost too much to bear, and the tears were shed, and yet you have come through all of those with new vision to a place where you stand right now on the threshold of realizing your Christhood, the Christ power. You stand just this side of truly coming alive in the Christ. Hear me well. Hear me well and get excited about it.

Now, some of you have been thinking, "Well, that is okay for you, Jeshua; you know Christ. You lived through your challenges. For me, I am not so sure. I certainly don't want to have to go through what you did in order to realize my Christhood." I have said to you before, and I will say it again: you do not have to come through the physical crucifixion. Already in this lifetime you have been through the emotional crucifixion.

But I will share with you that the image of my life, the interpretation and the recording of it which you have in your holy Scriptures, does not tell the whole story. For in truth, I did not suffer as it has been written. In truth, I knew my Christ power and I was not afraid of it. You stand yet on the threshold; you stand with the foot raised ready, perhaps, to step over the threshold; and yet you say, "I'm not quite sure. What happens if I claim my Christhood and I take that step forward? Is it going to be too much? What will happen?"

I will share with you that there is absolutely no one or no thing that is going to keep you from stepping over that threshold; not even yourself, not even the separated ego. So you might as well go for it.

What it means to be Christ is not what has been recorded in your holy Scriptures. I knew human experience. I came and allowed a body to be the vehicle of language in that day and time. I came and was incarnate, activated the body the same as you. I also activated the emotions so that I would know, truly know, what the brothers and sisters in this reality experience.

You have heard it said, and it is a truth, that I am in charge of the Atonement. I am in charge of the Awakening, the Remembrance upon this plane. Now, how could I uplift others; how could I teach; how could I relate, give you information, pathways, avenues, ways of coming up over the constricted limited belief that this plane is based upon unless I experienced it myself? I chose to know human experience, the same as you have chosen.

The recording which you have in your Scriptures of my life and the supposed ending of my life tells only a partial truth, and it has been polished to suit certain ones' interpretation and certain ones' goals. Much of the story has been left out. My story, in truth, is your story as well.

I would do with you a meditation.

Allow the body to be comfortable. Take a deep breath and go within. Go within to that quiet place of the mind and visualize in the mind's eye the candle flame which burns eternally within you.

As you stare at the candle flame within your mind's eye, allow it to grow until it envelops all of the body—a radiant light glowing, pulsating, expanding. See it going beyond the boundary of your body until the whole room is filled with light, brilliant golden white light.

See the light enveloping the dwelling place and the countryside surrounding. See the light growing, expanding at the speed of light past our holy Mother, the Earth, out into all of the other universes as far as you can imagine. Allow yourself to ride the wave of light, a feeling of accelerated flow beyond any speed you have known for quite awhile.

Feel yourself transported in this wave of light. Know yourself to be as expansive, as large as the whole wave of light. Feel yourself to be so large that you do not know where the boundaries of this light are; for in Truth, there are no boundaries.

Feel yourself to be expanded light. The warmth of light. The radiance of light; unlimited, expansive, forever ongoing light. A space of consciousness, yes, for you are not lost. There is still the consciousness, the I Am-ness, beingness which we may identify as the individual or as the whole, the same as the drop of water within the ocean.

Within this unlimited, infinite sphere of light, there is all wisdom. There is all, everything. It is, in Truth, the sphere out of which you make your other realities.

Come with me now in that sphere to a reality where I as a beingness, an awareness, a consciousness which I have called my Self, met with other beings, individualized energy and wisdom, and played with ideas, watching a reality that a grouping has brought together, a reality that you know well as this plane of reality.

We, as we saw ourselves to be a collective council, agreed that there would be a time of enlightenment, a time of acceleration, remembrance, and we looked upon this plane of reality and we loved it. We loved the grouping, as ourSelves, which has brought it forth and has been playing in this reality.

There was a thought to infuse this reality with more light, enlightenment, if you will. The collective thought was that I would go into this reality, a reality that yet believes in darkness, and bring my light to begin a time of enlightenment. I agreed to do this in an instant of time outside of time, and it was considered how this would be accomplished within the collective grouping that had brought this reality forth. There was a scripting, a drama, if you will, and the ones known as Mary and Joseph, as you know them now, agreed in an instant outside of time that they would also be part of this new drama, this time of light.

So, within an instant outside of time, all was set in motion, and within the passage of time I came to be incarnate. I brought with me, by collective agreement, a great light which your wise ones called a star, and you were there.

I came with the remembrance of Light, of Christ power. It infuses all of the physical. I came with a remembrance of Love, and those who came into my presence felt an energy of love. As I grew to a young lad there was much that I remembered and brought forth upon this plane which came from the power of the Christ. You knew me. You played with me. You knew Mary and Joseph.

As I became the adolescent, there was much in my studies which related to this reality, for it was necessary that I take upon myself—as you have done—the cloak of humanhood; to know it intimately; to talk as a man; to live as a man; to feel as a man; and I knew human emotions.

I knew also a calling from the earliest time of the incarnation that there was a service to be done, and I manifested for myself opportunity to study in far lands, lands which had cultures and beliefs different from those of my home—small "h"—my homeland. I took upon myself the discipline of human experience. There was much of training, for, you see, I did not know human experience intimately that specific way, so there was training and challenge and discipline, the same as you have experienced even in this lifetime.

When I returned from the far lands, there was a growing awareness within me of the power of the Christ, an excitement, if you will, of wanting to share what I had put together from all of the disciplines and training. I wanted to share with the brothers and sisters a new world, a new kingdom—not a kingdom of the world, but a transformation—and I desired from the compassion of my heart to make things better for the brothers and sisters. I saw the suffering. I saw the hopelessness. I also saw the hope that wanted to be fanned as a flame into a great fire, the same as there is hope in this day.

I selected friends to walk with me, and wherever there was a chance, I spoke of the greater vision. I spoke of love. I spoke of healing. I encouraged ones to know the Father's love, to know that they were not forgotten. Many of you took it deeply to heart, and your lives were transformed.

I knew that the teaching which I brought was as a sword that would cut through the old beliefs, and I knew also that it was not going to be taken easily by those who were adhering to the old structure. I questioned of the Father, could I not collect to myself a grouping and go off into the mountains somewhere, establish a monastery and teach from there? You see, I knew human emotions. But the answer was that I was to be amongst the people—not to retreat, not to take myself apart, but to be amongst the people, the brothers and sisters—and so I walked among you and I loved and I touched; I encouraged, and I drew always from the power which I knew to be beyond this world.

There are times that I would take myself away from the multitudes to commune with the Father; to breathe, to breathe deeply of the peace and the power that is in the breath. It is the simplest of tools and yet the most powerful; this was one of the teachings which my masters taught me: the power of the breath. I communed momently with the Father.

I spoke to you, the friends of the Father, in order to bring you a closeness of understanding, to bring to you that place where you would understand a parent's love and care: not a God afar off, but a family, a loving parent, a Father who was all power to nurture, support. I spoke of the Father, "Abba," in a personal way, for I knew His love in a personal way, and I drew my strength from His love.

As I walked amongst you and shared simply what I knew in my heart—those years of what has been called my ministry—I grew in understanding. I came to a point of transformation, called the Transfiguration, when I knew the power and radiance of the light of the Christ. I knew myself as Light; not just as human being; not just as body; not just as individualized personality; but as Light. And I knew there was nothing which could extinguish or overcome that Light.

I took upon myself then in the moment of transfiguration the most wonderful love, and from that moment on, everything I did was done in love. Now, up to that point, I was in service in love: human love, compassionate love, brotherly love. But from the moment of transfiguration I lived in pure Love, so that when there came the time of the crucifixion, I did not feel it to be devastating.

Now, I will admit from the human viewpoint that I had questions of how I would come through this. I had had training and discipline, physical challenge, but not to the point of releasing the body; so I questioned. Then I took the deep breath and I remembered all of the light, the great sphere of Light, and I knew myself to be above and beyond all of the world's activity. I looked upon all with pure Love. You were there with me.

You took from that event much of your truth—small "t"—a truth which has influenced all lifetimes since then, and you have believed in the possibility of abandonment. You have said that even love could be temporal and passing and would not last, and that you could not trust love. You would armor yourself against it. You have taken many truths—small "t"—from those days.

You stand now in a most wonderful place of releasing the old beliefs which have hindered your remembrance, for, in Truth, I did not suffer. In Truth, I was in love and joy—transfigurative love and joy—where nothing appeared to me the same as it did to others witnessing the scene. When I had released the body and it was finished, I went again to the Light which I Am and you Are, into the great sphere of Light where you dwell always. I met with the council of friends, and there was great rejoicing.

Then there was thought to come once again, to be with you once again, to say that the releasing of the body was not the ending. It is but part of the experience of the holy Child. It is only an experience. It is not the ending. I came again in love and walked amongst you, and I come again in this day and I walk amongst you, for I love you.

Allow all of the limited beliefs, the constrictions, to dissolve away into the non-truth which they are. I am alive. I am well. I am with you always. I am the Christ of you. I am One with you. You can play at separation, but only for awhile. For truly, I stand at the door and knock, and it is time to allow me in. When I come in to sup with you, you will recognize me as your Self, the one true Self, the Christ, the friend, the brother, for I love you always.

Living In The Mind Of God

We have been speaking about how you live a miracle every moment in focusing upon this reality—small "r"—bringing a focus of attention so completely to this reality, this individuality, this personality, even the body which you claim as your own, that there is a temporary forgetting of the whole of you. We have spoken also of the interdimensional Self, the Self which is not focused upon a dimension: the interdimensional Self, the wholeness of you, the holy You, out of which you draw the energy to focus upon this part and to call it a reality.

We have spoken of various exercises of releasing specific focus. Now, I do not mean for you to lay down the body, but I mean for you to have the beholder's view in releasing the strong attachment to this dimension and this reality to the place where you can begin to understand and to experience the holy Self, the interdimensional Self, even in the midst of the intensity of this reality. We have spoken about focusing upon energy, so that instead of focusing upon bodies or personalities, you were seeing in the mind's eye the energy in the interchange of conversation, the interchange of ideas, the interchange of communication.

Now, why is this important? For several reasons, one being that sooner or later in this lifetime you are going to release specific focus upon this lifetime. You are going to allow the body to be cast off as a shell, a vehicle perhaps, and you are going to move into another dimension, as you call it, of Reality.

So that is *a* reason that I speak to you of moving into the place of beholder, moving into the place of releasing such specific focus on this reality. But that is not the main reason, for indeed, you have laid down the body countless times and you have done very well with it. You have not gotten lost in the big void somewhere, never to know yourself again. So that is not the main reason for our discussion of the topic.

The reason is so that you may have peace even in this lifetime, knowing that, "Yes, I am in the world. There are worldly activities which I must attend to. There is drama in the world. There is energy in the world that I am in association with, but I am not the world. I am in the world, but I am not the world. The world is of me. It is my creation."

The reason is so that you move into the place of the beholder in peace, which allows you the deep breath which we have spoken of oftentimes. It allows you the deep breath of peace; to stand back with new perspective, and then to proceed in this lifetime with a mellowness, not getting caught up in the constriction of appearances, which has been your habit, individually and collectively, for so many lifetimes.

We have spoken that this is a most wonderful lifetime, in that you are willing now to entertain the concept, the idea, that perhaps you are more than just the body. Perhaps you are more than the individuality and the personality. Perhaps there is more to life; and to take the nose out of specific focus far enough to be able to look around to see the horizon and what is on the horizon.

For many lifetimes there has been the collective belief that you had to preserve the body. That was the main focus: you had to do everything to serve the body. It kept you very busy in all of those lifetimes protecting the body, for there were then, as there are now, energies of creativity that would want to bring to your doorstep the possibility of drama, the possibility that your body would be asked of you, and so you developed a very complex system of armoring—both physical armoring of the body and emotional armoring—to avoid any possible threat to what you saw as *you*.

You have brought the memories of the necessity of armoring into this lifetime even within the cells of the body as a memory, as old wounds, limited beliefs which have shaped this lifetime. They have shaped what you have chosen to believe as truth and influenced how you have seen others and their interaction with you. But you have done a most wonderful miracle in this lifetime, for you have been moving to the point of saying, "Perhaps there is much more to me. Perhaps there is more to life than just satisfying the body and keeping the body alive; protecting it, feeding it, nourishing it, bringing forth new life as the small children. Perhaps there is more than just the nine-to-five job. Perhaps there is more than just satisfying the parents, the peers, society. Perhaps the inner Self of me is calling out to be heard. Perhaps the inner Self of me wants to be nurtured and acknowledged."

You have been listening to the inner Voice. You did not do this most other lifetimes. The belief, the possibility was not there. But in this lifetime—and indeed, you have planted the seeds for this lifetime in previous lifetimes—there has been a gradual fruition where you have said, "There *is* more. I know the inner Self of me is speaking Truth. I want to know more of my holy Self." And as you do that, you will behold miracles in your midst, for indeed, miracles are all around you.

The releasement—detachment it has been called in other philosophical lineage—from the very narrow, limited, specific focus upon this dimension is one of the ingredients in the new paradigm which you are bringing forth. For indeed, you are standing upon the threshold of a new time, a new era.

You are bringing forth a new paradigm, a new understanding of the expression of the creative holy Child. It is the acknowledgment of the Christ within. That Christ of you has been from before time began, and that Christ of you is going to see you through all of time into the new time, into the place where you move with the freedom which is not dictated by society or by time or by any of the arbitrary values which have been held to be truth—small "t"—up to this point.

It has seemed to be a gradual process, because that is how you have asked for it to be presented to you. But in Truth, you already know. There is a part of you which you desire to connect with which is already living in what you call the future. There is a part of you that you connect with in your quiet times known as meditation, a part of you that you connect with in your visioning, your times of releasing all of the limitations of "What might I experience? If I were totally free, if I were totally powerful as the Christ, what might I experience in the days to come?"

Now, where does that question come from? It comes from the holy Self of you which is already living in the future and would communicate with you as you see your point of focus being here and now in a more limited understanding and remembrance. So there is a part of you—not separate; it is very much connected to you by a silver cord of consciousness, so it is not out of your reach—which knows the future, as you call it, and knows the preparation you desire in order to walk into this new self of you, awake. That is what you are doing, and it is no small thing.

It is something you have been preparing for since the beginning of time, since the beginning when you said, "I will have an adventure. I will see what I can create. Being the child of my Father/Mother/the creative One, I want to know what I can bring forth to create. What can I experience?" And with that thought you have brought forth all worlds, all realities, all dimensions. You have brought forth many, many adventures, and you have lived the adventures over and over with slightly new nuances as to how to play the role, for you have wanted to understand creation and to understand manifest expression of the Christ energy intimately. You have wanted to know it from the inside out; therefore, you have created, and you have seen yourself on the outside looking in. But in Truth, you are the one on the inside who is creating.

Now you are coming to a place where you are acknowledging and claiming the whole. You are coming to the place
where you understand that you can place yourself outside of
anything and look in, or you can place yourself inside and look
out. You can see the perspectives from different vantage
points.

You do this in your quiet times of musing. You do this in
your times of creative thinking. You do this in your imagination. "What would it feel like if...? What would it feel like if I
were CEO of the biggest company that holds my interest?
How would it feel to have the power to direct energy, creative
energy, and have other ones join me in this creative adventure? How would it feel to experience the greatest love, to
know myself completely loved, accepted as I am; to even
celebrate it, fat thighs and all; to celebrate every cell of this
manifest body because I am wonderful? How would it feel to
be so loved that I am honored and celebrated as one of the
greatest masters who has brought his/her consciousness to this
plane?"

And so you have gone about understanding human love.
You have had relationships which have brought you to a
greater understanding of love in its human form. You have
done this because you have wanted to know expansion of Self
and to move into more of the remembrance of the true Being,
the expansive Being which you are.

You have played with all kinds of roles and scenarios:
"How would it feel to be the beloved pet? How would it feel
to be the bird, the eagle that flies so high? What would the
perspective look like from the eagle's point of view? What
does it feel like to swim in the ocean, to be one of the vast
creatures of the ocean? What does it feel like to dive to the

deepest place in the ocean and to see the mountains that are covered by water in this day and time?

"What does it feel like to travel to another planet? What does it feel like to be in conversation with space brothers? What do they have to tell me? More to the point, what do I have to tell them?" For it is always a two-way street. So you play with creative unlimitedness even within the concepts of limited remembrance of the holy Self, and as you play with creative unlimitedness, you move more and more into understanding the holy Self and remembering how it feels to be Christ.

Truly, you are moving into a new age, a new time when you are going to live from the Mind of God; not the human mind as you have understood it to be, but the human mind that knows itself to be an extension of the Mind of God. That is what you are moving towards. That is what you desire to experience and know, so that you no longer feel separate, feeling, "Here am I, and God is somewhere out there. Perhaps if I say the right words, if I say the right prayer, perhaps if I do the right ritual, then He will look with favor upon me." That has been the belief down through generations of time, but now you are moving into the space of understanding that, "I am an extension of the Mind of God. I am an extension of the Father brought, because of my choice, into this reality to serve Him."

Now, how do you serve the Father? It is by being in fully awakened consciousness, the light in a place which still believes in darkness.

The Mind of God has been spoken about for eons of time. It has been defined by your religious/philosophical lineages of thinking in many different ways according to societies and cultures. It has often been most mysterious, never to be defined in a way that you could quite grasp it. It was always something beyond the human mind.

Now in Truth, the Mind of God is the interdimensional Self of Reality—capital "R"—of you. It is the vast ocean of Beingness, of Consciousness, of Energy, out of which you draw the energy to make this reality, this dimension. You are not separate from the Mind of God. You use the energy of God, of Christ, to fashion the experiences that you have in every drama, in every adventure, this lifetime and every other lifetime.

The Mind of God is, yes, beyond what you see as human mind, because you have circumscribed what you have said human mind can encompass, what human mind can think about and realize. The Mind of God is beyond, yes, because it is all this and much, much more, and you are not separate from it.

This is my gospel to you: you are not separate from the Mind of God. You have never been separate. You cannot be separate from the Mind of God. You cannot be outside of the Mind of God even as you temporarily believe yourself to be outside of it, and as you claim experiences which you define then to be outside of the Mind of God. But in Truth, you are never outside of or abandoned by or forgotten by God, the Father/Mother, the God Mind.

As you are now practicing moving into the space of beholder, as you are now practicing moving into the space of the interdimensional Self, you are moving into a remembrance and a realization of the God Mind. Do you see why we have been doing this in steps? Do you see why we have been gently, and yet with purpose, leading you, exhorting you even, to move into an expanded understanding of Self? It is to move you into the space of God Mind, for that is the Mind out of which you create; even the creations that you would say you did not want to own, the creations of which you would say, "I don't know how these experiences came to me. I didn't ask for them." Well, yes, you did, and you have created all that which you have experienced—loving and unloving—out of the energy of the interdimensional Self, out of the energy of God Mind.

You are the ones who have then labeled what you have created and called it either good or not so good, or sometimes horrific. But the God Mind only looks upon what you create and sees it as creative, sees it as energy that is being shaped and molded. It does not value judge. You are the ones who place value upon persons, things, events; and more often than not, you find yourselves lacking or you find others lacking, and you judge everything on a scale of being most wonderfully perfect to the place of being terrible, positively the worst, a hell on Earth. But the God Mind does not value judge. The God Mind *Is*.

You have your writings that have said that the God Mind is Love. You have your writings that say that God the Father/Mother is Love and is loving. There is truth in this but not the way that human understanding would define Truth. For human understanding, again, will take but a part of the whole. The Truth is that God Mind is Love as you understand love to be expansive and without limits.

We have spoken in other times of the feeling of human love, how it feels to be in human love. You fall totally, totally in love with someone or something or a beloved pet, and you are so in love with that one that you feel yourself to have released all boundaries. You feel expansive in that love, and for a moment or longer you lose all sense of the small self through the identification with the other one in love. Love is expansive. And the God Mind is expansive. It is love, yes, as you understand love, and yet more. It is expansive, forever ongoing, forever expressing Itself even beyond time. To use the word forever still connotes some time, and the God Mind, the Isness of you, is forever and forever ongoing beyond time. You have taken a segment of the God Mind and put it within an understanding of time. Even as you would see time as being most vast upon this plane, it is still but a segment, if you will, within the creativity of the God Mind.

You are functioning within that segment, and for many lifetimes you have said, "This is all I can be." But now you are moving into a place of claiming and connecting with the God Mind, the Allness of You, and it will not blow the circuits. That has been a fear of the separated ego. Now, it will blow the separated ego, but it will not blow the circuits of your consciousness to the place where you will lose yourself. You will never lose the individual consciousness of you as you know yourself to be individuality unless you choose to meld with more of the holy Self of you and to identify with that Self.

Anytime you want to connect with the individuality that you claim to be you, the individual consciousness of you in any lifetime, any dimension of expression, it is available to you. There is a belief within the paradigm of the collective consciousness of this time and space that you are cut off from all but what may be a very small bit of what you call past lives, and even those you are not quite sure of.

You go to psychics, you go to ones who you say have a bit more of the vision, and you say, "Who have I been in past lives?" They give you a tidbit, and you say, "Well, yes, that feels true for me," and you claim it, and yet there is a question mark in the mind that says, "Well, I'm not quite sure," because the collective consciousness has dictated that "This is all there is that I will know about myself, just this very specific point of focus right here." But in Reality, you can always call up in your consciousness any individuality and any individual consciousness which you claim to be *you* in any expression, any lifetime, any dimension, and you can experience that individuality. It is not separate from you; as the God Mind is not separate from you.

As you will go about your daily living there is a tool, a way to become more mindful of the God Mind, and it is to be mindful of what you are doing in every moment. I watch you—you and the brothers and sisters—as you go about your daily activities, and so much of the time you have a focus of interest in the past, what has happened an hour ago, a day ago, a week ago, even years ago; or you have the focus of interest in the future, what you are going to experience in the next day, the next week, in the next year; how you are going to write the next report; how you are going to talk with someone about whatever; where you are going to travel, etc., and so little of your focus of attention is placed upon the present moment and being mindful in that moment of where you are and what you are doing.

So I would suggest unto you, as you will want to connect more and more with the God Mind, that you begin connecting with the mindfulness of what you are doing in every moment. Where are you right now? Be mindful of that. How does it feel to be where you are right now? What do you see? What do you experience? What are you taking into the human mind and interpreting?

A life of mindfulness is the foundation of moving into the remembrance of God Mind. I would suggest to you not to spend so much energy on the past or on the future, but to bring the focus into the here and now, the joy of the here and now. For indeed, if you have been carrying a heavy burden, being worried about some situation, if you feel that there is something that you need to do to set something right or you have some fear, perhaps, I ask you, where is that worry right now? Where is that fear? Where is that event or situation you are contemplating? It exists in the past or in the future. But right now, as you take a deep breath, you are living in the present moment in peace. Right now, if you take a deep breath, you can allow the body to release all of the constriction, all of the fear and worry that you carry in the solar plexus. You can allow the belly to be soft; you can allow the heart to open; you can allow the lungs to expand, to breathe in a most wonderful inspiration and to dwell in peace this moment. Be mindful of where you are in this moment.

Do not put yourself forward in time, for indeed, when you reach the place where you have to deal with something that you see as being in the future, you will deal with it easily.

The separated ego has said unto you so many lifetimes that you have to prepare, that you have to be ready to defend, to take care of the body, to take care of the emotions even. The separated ego has said, "You must walk down every possible road ahead of time. You must look around every corner. You must look under every stone and rock to see what might be hiding there. You must rehearse what you are going to say, etc."

I see you as you allow the mind to fast-forward and you rehearse: "What am I going to say? Should I say this? How will they accept it? Maybe I should say...," and you spend a lot of energy in a future time that may not even happen. Be mindful of the present, of where you are right now in the present. Breathe deeply of the peace of the present moment and the gift that is in the present moment.

One of the reasons you call it the present is because it *is* a gift. Allow yourself as the holy Child to accept the gift and to live in the present. If there are things that you have to do for an employer that move you to a goal in the future, then attend to them in the present, but be mindful of living in the present even as you know you are preparing for a time which seems to be in the future. Do not put yourself into the future in a way which constricts all of the life flow to the place where you do not have joy of living. Abide in the present. Be mindful that, "Yes, I am working on a report which has to be given some days from now, or I am working on a project with someone else that will be called together at a later time. I am mindful that I am working on that and I am mindful that I am in the present right now."

As you will draw the focus of attention to the mindfulness, the awareness of where you are right now, you will find that there is a gifting of peace which allows you to move into the claiming and the realization of the God Mind which is always at work, even when you have said, "I am separate from the God Mind." As you are mindful—lower case "m"—it allows you opportunity to move into the remembrance and realization of the one Mind—capital "M"—the place which knows detachment, which knows, "I am *in* the world, but I am not *of* the world. I have a purpose and reason for being here. But the reason for being here is not to be so constricted that I am not in joy with living. The reason and purpose is to be the joy of the Father incarnate and to live from that space as the holy Child."

Why do I call you "child"? It is to tickle the remembrance of how it feels to be innocent, how it feels to be the child who is spontaneous about life, who does not have to rehearse, does not have to think how everything is going to be.

Now, as the child grows a bit in stature, it takes on a bit of the "wisdom of the world." It is not true wisdom. The child, the innocent holy Child, becomes the adaptive child, for the child adapts itself to what it believes is going to be expected of it, what is going to bring love, reward.

But the holy Child, the innocent holy Child of you, is the Child which goes spontaneously, is excited about life, wants to have adventures just for the fun of having adventures, wants to see, "What is this new land? What do the mountains look like? What do the waters look like? What new formation am I going to see? What wondrous formation have I brought forth? I, as the creative one in co-creating all of this manifest expression of energy upon this plane, want to see that. I want to experience it, and I have the courage to go ahead and do it." Your dreams are still alive and well, and as long as you draw breath, go, experience. Know that you have the experiences that you bring forth out of the Mind of God because you are an extension of God the Father/Mother. For so many, many lifetimes you have bought and paid dearly for the truth—small "t"—that this was all there is, and that you were not worthy to experience anything better; that you were not even worthy to pray unto the Father. That has been a belief in many lifetimes. You had to have someone else who was closer to God to pray for you. You, lowly sinner that you were, were not even allowed to contemplate God, for if you contemplated God, surely you would die, because you could not hold a holy thought. You had been cast out of the Garden, out of the Kingdom, because of original sin, which you never understood anyway. You have believed, "I've been told I am very sinful. I am guilty of a horrible sin that originated before I even have any understanding, and I don't know the Father.

Therefore, I will seek someone else who has His ear and perhaps then I will be taken care of. I do have desires, but I won't speak them." This is how you have gone in other lifetimes. "I have desires but I can't speak them, because to speak them would be a sacrilege."

Well, now that idea seems a bit foreign to you. Praise God, the Self of you that it is, for you are moving into the place of remembering and claiming the holy Self, the sacred Self of you that can never be sacrilegious. You are moving into a place of great power; not as the world defines power, but the great place of Christ power, of creative power which comes from the power of the God Mind.

My message to you is to be mindful of the present moment. Do not dwell in the past. Do not dwell in the future. Allow yourself to be mindful of the present, and in the peace of the present acknowledge that, "I live and move and have my being in the God Mind. I am not separate from the Mind of God. It is not something that is mysterious and far removed from me. It is that which allows me to have the creative experience called this lifetime."

For indeed, a mindful life, where you are mindful of the present, is one which leads you to the happiness of knowing your connection with All That Is, that which has been called the Mind of God. The new time you are moving into is a time of miracles. It is a time which has not been defined yet. That is why your prophecies do not speak of it. You have not defined it yet, because it is going to be an open-ended experience even yet within time, because you have said you want to have this experience within the concept of time. But you are also going to know the timelessness of yourself.

You will define the new consciousness. It has not been written yet. That is what is most wonderful. You will define it because you are knowing now that you call forth the Christ energy from the Mind of God in order to fashion, and you will make it most wonderful, each and every one of you in your own unique way. Some will have visions of meeting with space brothers, of traveling to other universes, and those will be realities—again, small "r". Some will have experiences within that are so blissful that nothing in the outer will matter at all, for you have reached the place of great revelation, "I Am that which I Am, and I need no more."

You will move into most wondrous technology, because already you have set that in motion. You will move into the most wonderful inventions, both physical and energetic inventions. You will move into the space of knowing the heart of a brother, sister.

You will know the releasement of boundaries of small self, and you will bring forth a world which moves on the energy of love rather than keeping itself constricted by the energy of fear. You will define this new age out of the God Mind.

I speak to you as you move forth now into a new time, and I say to you, you will define that which seems to be undefinable, unimaginable in this moment, and you will define your reality—your most wonderful beautiful garden of reality—out of the energy of the Mind of God, the God Mind, and you will do it with the awareness that, "I Am that Mind."

Go forth, adventure, live, create, celebrate, and honor the God Mind, and know that always I walk with you into the remembrance of the One Self.

So be it.

In My Father's House...

I would speak with you now about that which you find in this reality to be both promising and challenging. I would speak with you about life, and death, as you call it. In each lifetime you have the promises of the new lifetime as it is begun, as the small one is birthed, and in each lifetime you have the challenges of understanding the releasement of the body, yours and the loved ones.

You have a saying within your Scriptures which has been attributed to me—and I did say it—that in my Father's house are many mansions. By that I meant that in the Reality of the

Father there are many dimensions, many realities, many mansions—or perhaps sandboxes—to play in, and this includes many lifetimes.

For the Father would not limit you to just one lifetime. The Father does not limit. Your divine teacher does not limit. You are limitless. In my Father's house are many mansions, many ideas, many realms, many places to adventure; not only the physical location places, but places within the mind and the imagination to adventure.

You have fashioned for yourselves, over and over, many different mansions to play within, many different lifetimes. Oftentimes you have asked of companions, ones of the soul group, the vast soul group, to be with you once again upon the stage of another lifetime. You meet once again, playing different roles, having different scripting, and you play to each other.

Each lifetime, no matter how you fashion it, is full of promise. Every moment, in truth, is full of promise. It awaits your command. A lifetime is very flexible, malleable; you can change it, can mold it to be what you want it to be and do. You make changes within an instant. You make a shift in perception and suddenly everything looks different, and suddenly you are different.

Each one who claims a physical lifetime is a master. All, in Truth, are equal. All are of the Father from before time began. All have their own choices and desires to fulfill. Some will fulfill what they see a lifetime purpose to be in a short time. Some will garner many years to themselves before they release the body. There is no judgment as to whether one releases the body at what would be seen as an early time or a later time.

It is not to be said that some are more efficient; therefore, they get done faster and that there is value judgment in that, and there is not a value judgment that says those who release the body at an early age have lost anything, because, in truth, you cannot lose anything.

One comes into a lifetime with a generalized pattern of a goal, a purpose of that lifetime, within a broad generalization. Within that broad generalization there is very much room for improv and specifics, because the holy child is creative at all times. But for each and every one who desires and claims a lifetime, there is an overall goal, certain issues perhaps to be seen in holiness, to be understood, to be known intimately to the place of completion.

It is said that you come into the world alone and that you exit the world alone, but that is not true. You do not come into the world alone. There are many angels attending the birth of every small one, and there are many angels attending every step of your lifetime. When you release the body, you are welcomed into a loving group of guides, teachers, angels, loved ones whom you will recognize and feel very much at home with, very much welcomed.

You have had some accounting of this where ones have had the near-death experience, where they have felt such a welcome, such a peace, such a joy that when they were given instruction that perhaps it was not quite time to release the body and that they must "go back," there was not a desire to come back to the physical lifetime.

When the focus upon the body is released, there is a welcoming by ones you will recognize. I will be there and you will recognize me. The loved ones who have released the body ahead of you, as you measure time, will be there to meet you, even if they have, in their most extended state, focused upon another incarnation. They are not limited to just the one focus upon the incarnation. They will be there to meet you.

The releasing of the body is, in truth, a completion. It is a graduation. Now, for the ones who are left seemingly without the companionship of that one activating a body, there is a time of adjustment. But in truth, you gift yourself every experience, and the experience of another one's releasing the body is a gift that you give to yourself to move into expanded understanding of Self—Self with a capital "S," but also self with a small "s,"—to understand that even the self—small "s"—as you see yourself to be individual is not confined just to personality or to body or even to specifics of a lifetime. The Self of you is very much expansive. The Self of you is what you have called the soul.

Now, as you understand self, you say, "Well, I am myself. I am an individual. I am known by a certain name. I have certain attributes. People recognize me. They call me by my name, and that is my individual, individuated self." But there is more to yourself than just the individuated expression, and the more is the soul of you.

The soul of you is the repository of all of the experiences of all of the lifetimes you have ever imagined for yourself. It is as you would see a certain memory, a record if you will, of where you have been, who you have been, what you have felt, what you have experienced, what you have given and received in all lifetimes in this dimension, this reality, and all others as well. So you can see that the soul of you is quite expansive.

As you follow the soul back further in the stream of Beingness you come to spirit, the divine Isness of you out of which you have fashioned the soul and out of which you have fashioned the individuated expression.

To put that in another way, there is the Isness of you which you cannot even comprehend. It cannot be conceptualized. The Isness just Is. Within the vastness of Isness, of Being, you as the creative one, the Child of the one Creator, not separate from, but as an ongoing extension of the vast Isness, the creative Isness, have fashioned a consciousness which you call the soul, which you call your Self. The soul then is who and what you have ever been, who and what you will ever be—you keep adding to it—and who and what you know yourself to be in the present moment, which allows you to come to the most miraculous singular focus, to this individuated experience which you call yourself right now.

Many have asked what the soul is. Many have asked what the difference between spirit and soul is. You are spirit, and out of spirit you have fashioned for yourself seemingly unique experiences which you claim for your Self, and I say *seemingly* because you are as a drop of water in the ocean which sees itself to be separate as a drop of water, and yet it is the ocean as well.

But for the experience and the expression of a unique consciousness you have fashioned a soul history for yourself. Most wonderful. This is why there are ones who know me in a certain incarnation as one Jeshua. Others know me by other names: Sananda, Raj Pur, Archangel Michael. Am I all of these ones? Yes, as you claim for yourself a certain lineage of soul history.

There is a most wonderful promise which you made to yourself from before time, because time is a relatively new thing, to speak of it within the concept of time. It is a relatively new thing. It is not within all dimensions. It is not within all realities, but it is within this one. Before time, before you even thought that there might be process—a beginning, middle, and end that would be marked off as time—you made a promise to yourself, and the promise was to go where no consciousness had yet gone; to know Creation in its holiness, in its wholeness—all of it—and to, in Truth, live to the fullness. Whether it be activating a body or not, that is not important. What is important is awareness. It is consciousness. It is the Isness, divine Isness. Whether you do that with a body or whether you do that without the pleasure and/or hindrance of a body, in Truth, matters not.

Life is full of promise, full of gifts. Death as you look upon it is also full of promise and full of gifts. I would have you understand more fully the process of life and death. For truly, you have come through many lifetimes where you have been born and where you have released the body, where you have been the small one who brought great joy to a family, where you have been the small one who brought great consternation to the family. You have been the aged wise one who was revered, and you have been the aged wise one who has been the outcast. In other words, you have lived all of the scripting.

The point I am making is that you have known life and seeming death over and over to the place where you come in this lifetime wanting to truly understand it; not to hold the death idea away from you, saying, "I'm not going to look at it because I am afraid of it. Maybe it won't happen." Well, I have news for you. It does happen. It will happen. It comes right to your consciousness. But the gifting in it is to know that you have invited it to come, to know that you are strong enough—because you have invited it—to deal with it and to gain from it and to be in joy about it; to celebrate each passing, birth and death, as a graduation.

Chapter 8

What you are striving to do as a whole holy Child is to come to a balance and understanding that the birthing is a gifting and the releasement is a gifting and that Life itself is eternal; it is ongoing. This point of reality, wonderful though it is, is not the only point of reality. In my Father's house are many mansions.

Therefore, I say to you, look upon each day, when you first open the eyes, as a birthing, for it is. It is a new day. You are as a new person as you open the eyes the first thing in the morning. Look upon that as a birthing of that day and yourself in that day, and when you come to the evening and you lay the head upon the pillow, allow that to be the releasing of the focus upon the body; not to the place where it is permanent releasing, but to the place where you allow yourself peaceful repose. You do this every night anyway, and it is no big deal. When you come to releasing the body, it will not be a big deal either.

For those who are left to care for the shell, the vehicle, the body, gift to them before your releasing a word to the wise that you will always be with them; that you are not the body. Write out for them certain instructions which will help them deal with the shell, the vehicle, the body, because at a time like that there are emotions which come up, and the loved ones do not always know what to do. So give them the gift of writing what you want done with the cast off body, and speak to them that Life is eternal. Speak to them that which you know in your heart. Tell them true the experiences you have known in the lifetime which have proved it to you so that they are not left bereft, cast adrift without an oar. Give them an oar or two.

Then when you come to the place of releasing the body, you will go with joy, knowing that you have completed.

Wonderful, beloved holy Child of the Father, celebrate life, celebrate death, celebrate the Self, and know that always you are loved.

So be it.

The Nature Of Reality

Now, beloved one, I would speak with you about the nature of Reality. You have a reality which you share with the brothers and sisters, a reality which says, "I am activating a body. I am in a certain geographical location. It is a certain time of the day. It is a certain day of the month, etc." This is a reality which you have agreed upon.

Your reality is based upon a collective core belief, first of all, as to incarnation—what it means to be incarnate within this reality—and there is a collective consciousness which defines the reality of this particular form of incarnation.

In truth, the incarnation which you make for yourself within this reality is not the only form of incarnation which you can have, have had, will have. There are many forms of incarnation; this is but one. It is called human, and it is most wonderful. It is a miracle what you bring forth in this incarnation: to coalesce light, a physical energy of light, into a certain density of form which you then perceive with physical receptors known as the eyes. Even as you look upon brothers and sisters, all of the forms, although human, are different.

Some are very much alike, the ones which you call the identical siblings, identical twins, but even those ones the parents can tell apart for there are differences, much the same as you acknowledge that every snowflake is different. Most wonderful miracle. You call forth from your creativity within the collective agreement of physicality a certain form to play with in a lifetime. You coalesce light into a certain density of vibration which allows you movement, sensation. You play with this certain form for a lifetime, and then by choice you recycle and incarnate again if you want to, in human form or in another type of incarnation. Some of the forms which you activate in other dimensions, other realities, are very different from the density of this form. Some are light as gossamer, much as you would call your certain emanations of ghosts. Some are quite fluid as you would understand the liquid form to be as it flows; it has certain form, but is more amorphous than what you see this density of form to be.

You as the holy Child have brought forth in your universes many realities where there are life forms; some similar to what you activate here on our holy Mother, the Earth; some which are dissimilar; some forms which live within the planets; some within the stars; some which live within the non-space between the bodies in the universe. There will come a time, if you see yourself yet to be activating human form, when you will have expanded sensory capability to know and communicate with the forms which are in the space and the non-space between bodies.

So, as you can see from this slight introduction, there are many realities—small "r"—this one being one that you have agreed you will play with. The collective consciousness called "human" says there will be certain physical laws which govern how the incarnated bodies work and how everything else with which you populate your world will work in conjunction and in connection with the physical body. For example, the chairs that you put the body upon are energy coalesced into form at a different vibratory rate so that you can sit upon them. The same with your dwelling place. You have certain walls, and if you want to walk through the transparent wall, otherwise known as the sliding glass door, you find that it is difficult within the collective agreement to walk through that transparent wall. Something about vibratory rate is different. You learn at a very young age what the physical laws are that govern the human incarnation, and your perception of the laws defines your reality—small "r."

You have, first of all, within the collective consciousness and the collective agreement a broad reality that you function within. Within that broad reality you have other realities, sub-realities defined by culture and society. You learn as a small one from the close family, the parents and the siblings, what the agreed upon reality is as you are growing in stature and wisdom.

The shared reality of family varies, as you have seen, from family to family, and when there is the intermarriage of one family with another there is, hopefully, a marriage of realities. Oftentimes this requires a bit of adjustment, trying to fit two similar, but not the same, realities together.

You have a shared reality of the family. You have a shared reality with the parents, with the siblings, and with the playmates as you are growing a bit taller. You have a shared reality in the schooling, wherever you take your schooling. All of this shared reality defines your reality and how you see it. Within your own individual reality there is much that defines it according to your perception of what you have experienced within the collective consciousness, within the family group, within the interaction with siblings and playmates, within your interaction with so-called authority figures, your perception of how you have functioned and do function in relation to others in this shared reality. Your individual reality is defined by your beliefs and perceptions, collective and individual, throughout this lifetime and other lifetimes as well.

For when the small one agrees to incarnate and comes as the infant, this one comes already with memories, already with certain issues that they desire to play with, to know intimately, and to see in holiness—eventually or perhaps sooner—in a lifetime.

Every small one, as you have witnessed, comes with a different set of memories from other lifetimes which shape from the very first moment the reality of that one. Those of you who have witnessed siblings within a family and have seen the small ones at birth and shortly thereafter as they were growing, you see that no two are alike. Even the ones that we spoke of that would be the identical siblings are not the same in appearance, in form, and they are not the same with regard to personality and perception of their reality, and this becomes even more defined as time goes on.

Your reality has many aspects, components which shape it, define it, and it is being shaped and defined moment by moment. It is a work in progress, open to improv every moment. All of a sudden you get a revelation, and what seemed a moment previous to be a very true—small "t"—reality—small "r"—is seen a bit differently, and you have a new reality for yourself.

Your reality—small "r"—is what you make of it. Now, you have the saying that you make your own reality, and you do. You shape it moment by moment based on your beliefs: core beliefs which you share with the collective consciousness and beliefs which you have brought with you from many lifetimes about what it means to be human; what it means for you individually to be human. And your reality is based upon specific individual beliefs which you hold in a certain lifetime.

So, when you have something coming up in your reality, ask of yourself, "What is the belief that supports this? Is it a belief that I gained from my parents, from the grandparents, from my playmates, from society? Where does this belief come from? Why do I believe it?"

Begin to be very aware of your reality and the underlying beliefs. It will give you revelation. It will give you opportunity to know freedom, for you will begin to see how your reality—small "r"—has been shaped down through the ages by what you have, up to this point in your reality, called "outside forces," and yet if you will begin to examine those "outside forces," you will see that you have agreed to every one of them because you have agreed to the incarnation.

You will see that by that agreement you are part of the collective which has said, "We will play within a certain sandbox together, and we will have certain rules about how we play in this sandbox." You have agreed that you will play for a time just for the fun of it, just for the creativity of it, just to see what you can make of the sandbox itself. For truly, the reality of the sandbox is not set. It is open to improv by the holy Child.

Now, regarding some of the core beliefs, you say, "Well, I can't change those. As long as I am going to be incarnate, there are certain core beliefs about what it means to be incarnate that I have agreed to." This is true momentarily, but there is also an evolution of the reality that is going on, so that in time—and it will not be that long a time—the ones incarnating will look at what you call reality now and will have a different view of what human incarnation means.

I will allow you to contemplate that thought, beloved one.

So be it.

The Healing Consciousness

Beloved one, you are standing now on the threshold of a time of great healing, for your world is calling out for transformation. The brothers and sisters are calling out for hope, for comfort, for something to believe in beyond the seeming random acts and chaos which they see in their world.

You, beloved one, can speak of hope. You have felt the joy within which the world does not understand, and you can say that even though appearances are most tragic, "I know Who holds me—and the future." It is not so much a "Who" as a

"What": the ongoingness of the Christ, the Love of Christ, and the divine order of the outworking of the Christ Love.

Now, in the day and time which you shared with me—that which is recorded in your holy Scriptures—a good percentage of my ministry dealt with healing, and much of my ministry had to do with teaching. In truth, all of my ministry had to do with teaching/healing, for you cannot separate the one from the other. As there would be teaching, and as it will be received and understood to the place of catalyst for remembrance, then comes forth healing.

How did I facilitate healing? First of all, we will start with the most obvious factor. There had been numerous examples of healing and miracles of healing so that there was a certain reputation which had been built up which gave credence to ones believing that I had special powers. So when they came into my presence there was already the belief that they could find a healing magic.

There was also within my presence a *knowing*, for I knew that these ones were already perfect, already healed, and that they could manifest the healing. So there was a reputation that went before me and there was also the magnetic energy field around me, because I knew that there was holy energy within me and within the others. I knew that all that was required for the healing to manifest was a certain connection, the same as you have in this day and time with your electricity. There is a possibility of electricity in the wire. There is the possibility of electricity in the outlet. You put them together and what happens? Great energy. But you have to put them together. It is the same with the magnetic healing energy, which you are. There is magnetic healing energy around you. It is the Life force. It is the Christ. It is the Isness which activates the body.

As you will desire to facilitate for others their remembrance of healing, you will do within yourself a certain amplification of Truth, of healing energy. It is a vibration of *knowing*, an Isness of *knowing*.

First, you acknowledge that there is an appearance of a problem. Then you draw your awareness, your point of focus, away from the obvious appearance. Now, this pertains to healing of the body and also for circumstances. You will draw your focus away from the appearance, and you will take yourself into the place of the beholder and look through the eyes of the Father. Take a deep breath. Remove the specific point of focus. You can still be looking at whatever concerns you, but within your consciousness raise up the consciousness to the place of expanded awareness of the energy of that one who is activating the body. Move your consciousness into the interdimensional Self, the Matrix of you, the holy Self of you.

In other words, you are going to forget your small self, because if you stay in the consciousness of your small self, that small self is going to say, "I can't do this." Well, that little "I" is not going to do it. But allow yourself to move into the place of the beholder, the interdimensional Self, to look through the eyes of the Father, if you will, to the energy, the Christ energy and also to the physical energy of the one or circumstance which would be healed.

Imagine the physical energy, first of all. If you do not see the energy with the physical eyes, imagine it within on the inner plane of your consciousness. You will see the person not as the physical body, but as the energy of vibration. You will see it swirling around the body, and you may see it in certain patterns. This is how you read the chakras. This is what you have done in other lifetimes when you have facilitated healing: you have read the energy vortices of all of the body, and

113

you have seen where there may be a certain vortex which has slowed down to the place where it is not allowing the light of the vibration of energy to circulate freely.

Then from the place of beholder you consciously direct the energy of the Christ Self through you to certain vortices to activate them—still from the place of beholder, because your part in this is to know their holiness; it is not to heal them. It is their choice whether they will plug into it or not.

There were ones who came to me who did not plug into the remembrance and were not healed. Was I a failure? No. Were they a failure? No. It was just a "No, not yet" decision. And you allow them the experience.

So you offer them the Christ energy from the place of the beholder and then you breathe and you smile. Whatever happens is okay. Then you walk on to the next one. I was always available, either in person or always in spirit, for ones who desired healing. There were ones who came to me and wanted to be healed in their awareness as self, individualized self. They wanted to be healed, and yet at another level there was meaning and purpose for the "No, not yet" answer.

But there came a later time when they called out to me and I was not there in physical presence, but they called out to me and said, "Aha, now I get it." And in that moment of the revelation there was healing.

So it does not have to happen in the very time when you, perhaps, want to see the results. It does not have to happen in your presence. Your job is only to be the willing Servant, to come from the place of the interdimensional Self, the Christ Self, the beholder, and with sincere desire to bring of the Father all the Love which the other one already is for the purpose of knowing holiness, for the purpose of healing.

The principle of healing is true when you are dealing with the body and it is also true for circumstances, relationships, and events. When you will hear of wars and rumors of war, allow yourself first of all the deep breath. Go into the place of the interdimensional Self, the Christ Self. Allow your consciousness to rise up. You may still be aware of events which are taking place on the world plane, but you are also taking your consciousness into the uplifted state of the Christ consciousness. Then look at the most wonderful dance—for that is what it is—which is being done. Watch the energy of vibration in the dance. Watch how it swirls. Look through the eyes of the Father and know that all serves the Atonement.

Each and every one of you has come once again into this lifetime to be a healer. Many of you have chosen, either as a direct profession or as an avocation, to be a facilitator of healing. Those of you who have not felt called in a direct way to be a healer are healers because of what you are living. As you are living from the space of optimism, of hope, the place of believing in the good, the place of loving, the place of friendship, the place that says, "Yes, you may fall down many times but I will be here to lift you up," you are healers.

You are a healer and this is a time of healing. It is a time when all of the issues which come from a place, a belief, unlike Love are going to come up to be looked at once again and to be transformed, to be seen in holiness and healed.

The human ego is calling out for healing. The human ego has lived in separation for so long that it calls out now to be lifted up into the Ego—capital "E"—the I Am Ego. The human ego is going to give you all kinds of questions, all of the "what if's" and the "buts," but in truth, the human ego is calling out now to be healed.

This is a time of healing and you are a healer, and I speak to you now as many of the beloved brothers spoke to you in what you would see as an earlier time, a time when you experienced being in the early groupings known as the early churches. You have recorded in your holy Scriptures letters which were written to you—for you were there as a member of one of the early churches. You did not see yourselves as an organization, as a church. You met in homes. You met in fellowship. You met in love, and you wanted to know then, as you have been asking in this lifetime, "What more is there to life?"

I would speak to you now of the healing of the soul. For indeed, all healing of the body is as an effect, a final result, of the healing of the soul: the releasement of old burdens from limited beliefs carried in other lifetimes, the releasing and the healing of old wounds.

I would ask you, first of all, are you in a place now where you could use some help with something that is going on in your life? If so, I have good news for you. There is help, and the help is all around you. Even as you look with physical eyes, the help is all around you. For as we spoke of how to facilitate healing of the body, now we will speak of facilitating healing of the soul: to be there—as it is in your common parlance—for another one; to be there in spirit and in love to support a brother, a sister in what they are going through and to facilitate for them the releasement of old baggage and the claiming of healing in the soul.

How do you do this? By true prayer together: the acknowledgement that you are not alone; the acknowledgement that, "I am always in the presence of pure Love and all help is available unto me at any time." As you will ask—even before—it shall be answered.

In this day and time there is a collective belief in separation. The collective belief says that there are separate bodies and that everyone goes his own way alone. There are many times when the separated ego will say to you that this is the truth of your being. It is not the Truth of your being—capital "T." It is a truth that you are living out—small "t"—because you have agreed that will be the paradigm of this time. And when you find yourself abiding in the space of separateness and aloneness, the world and all of its questions can feel very heavy. When you acknowledge, "I am not alone; I am in the presence of pure Love in this moment"—for in Truth, you are always in the presence of pure Love—"I am in the presence of the love of the guides and teachers and masters and angels, the saints and all of the loved ones that I have known any lifetime, past, present, future," then you take on a knowing of the greater Self and you walk with more confidence, for you have brought together more of the seemingly scattered energy of the holy Child. And when "two or more are gathered together in my name...;" in other words, when you call upon the seemingly separated and scattered parts of yourSelf there is great power, great healing power, great love.

When you find yourself desiring some support, call upon a friend. Call upon them first through the mind and through the heart, and then if you still do not feel their presence—and you will get to the place where you will call them with your mind and your heart and you will know they are instantly with you—then pick up your telephone and call and say, "I am facing a problem right now. I need some help. I need to know more of my holy Self. Will you be with me?"

And your friend or guide or guardian angel will say, "Of course. I am there for you. I have no other purpose in this lifetime"—which is true—"except to be with you in love." That is your purpose. And you will find in that moment a deep peace within and around you, and that which has seemed to be so sorrowful, so heavy, so conflicted will no longer feel so heavy, so sorrowful, so conflicting, for you have the power of the holy One joined together.

Now, I would suggest to you that as you describe to your friend or guide the challenge you are facing, you do not have to do a soap opera rendering of all of the details. Instead, when you speak with the friend or guide, put forth that which you desire to experience. That is the first step in the healing of the situation: the willingness to walk beyond that which you have found yourself mired in. For if you do a certain soap opera rendition, you only keep yourself and the other one in that space for a longer time. If you have to give some background, keep it abbreviated.

If you feel that you want the support of another one, do not put yourself down as being weak or being not quite good enough to do it all by yourself, but look around and find the holy Self of you incarnated as the brother and sister, and ask for support. You do not have to walk alone, for in Truth, never do you walk alone. Always I walk with you, but sometimes it is a little bit hard to hear my voice and it is easier to hear a friend's voice. Avail yourselves of that which is right here for you and allow it to be the pathway to the remembrance of the presence of pure Love. Pray for one another. Support one another. Be as described in the writing of my beloved brother, the one known as James, who said to you in a day and time long ago and says to you once again, "To pray for one another. To confess your faults one to another." By that he did not mean your shortcomings, but to state that which you have not yet seen in holiness; in other words, the problem; to confess, "I'm having a problem with..." whatever it is; and to support one another as your Father loves you.

Now, it is not necessary that the friend be incarnate. You may choose to call upon me or another master, guide, teacher, guardian angel. Pick up the spiritual telephone and know our Presence. Always I am with you.

So be it.

Healing Prayer

I am now in the presence of pure Love.
I acknowledge the presence of masters, teachers, guides,
  angels.
I acknowledge their love around me and within me.
I abide in the dwelling place of the Most High, for I am holy.

I invite and accept the support of the loving masters, teachers, guides, and angels in my life and affairs.
I invite and accept the support of all loved ones, here present
  or in other dimensions, in my life and affairs.

I desire to experience...(state what you desire to see healed
  in your life)...realizing that it requires I must release all old
  beliefs about this situation.

I breathe in the energy of divine consciousness within myself.
I breathe out all old beliefs I have held about this situation
  and condition. (Repeat as necessary)

I acknowledge the presence of divinity within me, my life
  and affairs.
I acknowledge that all is well.
I am at peace.

I give thanks that it is so.
And so it is.

The Way of the Master

Let us speak now about the way of the master. First and foremost, the way of the master is the way of peace. It is to choose to go within to the sacred place of peace which the world does not know: the peace that passes the understanding of the world. The world knows it not. But the way of the master is the way of peace, abiding in stillness and asking for holy vision: "How can I see this anew? What is truly happening; not just what I see as appearances, but what is truly happening? How can I behold it from a place of divinity and know my place in it?"

The way of the master is the way of the beholder. The way of the master is to take the deep breath, the physical deep breath and also the spiritual deep breath, and to choose to behold without judgment; not to have attachment to any of the outcome, because you cannot know, as you look upon the appearances, what is the highest and best outworking.

But as you go within to the place of peace, the place of the master within, you know you can trust. The way of the master is the way of trust, to trust that "that which I see is only part of what is happening," and to trust that all things work together for the awakening of the holy Child. The Awakening is truly what you have asked for, you individually and you as a collective. You have asked to come Home once again; to remember Who you are; to remember truly how loved you are; to know that, "I am loved of the Father; I am His Child; I am an extension of the divinity come forth into this plane to live a human life in all of its treasure." Human life *is* a treasure. Sometimes it is a challenge as you look upon it, but it is a gift. You are the extension of the Father come forth into this plane to live His life in a reality that is somewhat an adventure and to find joy in that adventure.

The way of the master is the way of love. It is to be the beholder and to look upon everything through the eyes of the Father, to look upon everything with love; not just human love--that takes you a certain distance and it is good--but to go beyond that to the place of divine Love.

Now, you know human love and you work with it as a symbol of the divine Love. When you fall in love with someone, you expand. Everything seems to take on more light. Everything in life seems to mean more. There is an exuberance, an exhilaration about life. You cannot wait to see the other one to share with them what has been going on. You cannot wait to live, to be truly alive.

Human love is but a part, a most wonderful clue, of divine Love. Fall in love everyday, please. Look in your mirror and fall in love with the one you see there. Have a most wonderful relationship with the one in the mirror. Begin to appreciate what you have brought forth as the creativity upon this plane. Come truly alive with it. Feel the vibration of life itself. See how wonderful it is to be alive and how you have chosen to express in this lifetime.

The way of the master is the way of beholding the Christ. It is the way of appreciating the beauty, the radiance of the Father's only Child, the holy Child, the Child of Love. You are a love child brought forth in Love.

The way of the master appreciates beauty. The way of the master knows that life itself is a beautiful gift. Never think that you have small meaning or that your life has small meaning. You have chosen out of great courage to be here upon this plane, for this is not the easiest reality. This is a reality which is based upon the belief in duality, the belief that there could be other than perfection, beauty, harmony, good. It believes that there could be separation from your divinity. You, as the adventurer which you are, have said, "I will go. Send me, Father. I will go one more time into that reality. I will assume the cloak of forgetfulness. I will say that I will walk the dream. And still, there will be a part of me which remembers, deep within me, a calling to come Home."

You have felt that calling, a deep Homesickness, a longing, a wanting to go Home, wanting to be held again in the arms of love--true Love, not conditional love. Some of you have made trek to your early childhood home, thinking, "If I go home again, it will be there for me." But you have gone to the early childhood home and it is not the same, and you did not find Home, for you will not find Home in the outer. It is only found in the inner. It is within you, and you carry it with you. Even the remembrance of the childhood home is within you, and you carry it with you. The way of the master recognizes the Home within and comes from the place of Home, the space of peace and completeness, lacking for nothing.

The way of the master is one of creativity; one which looks upon whatever is happening and asks, "What can I understand about this that is outside the box, outside of the usual way of understanding?" The way of the master is the way that looks upon things with new perception. The way of the master is the way that is willing to contemplate new ideas, new realities, new dimensions; to play with new possibilities even while walking within the old possibilities, probabilities, and realities.

I see you do this throughout your day. You do what is expected of you within what you have agreed to do, the reality you have agreed to, but part of you is somewhere else. Part of you is dreaming a most wonderful Real dream; not the dream of forgetfulness but the dream that is unlimited, the dream that plays with, "What if? What if all of the limitations were taken off? What if I could live with the physical body in its prime for as long as I wanted to? What if I had all of the golden coins to do whatever I want to do? What if an idea comes to me and I really could see it made manifest? What if I really could multiply the loaves and fishes?" And you can and do. You do not need another one with perhaps a bit more magic to multiply the fishes. I do not have more magic than you do.

Whatever you truly desire cannot be kept from you. It takes only your willingness to accept it. That is the way of the master: To believe, to know, to trust, and to go forward; to come truly alive; to live in peace as the beholder; to think outside of the box; to imbue everything you do with a divine energy of life—True Life, truly lived—and to live in the joy which that courage brings you; to come to a place of knowing, "I am my Father's Child; I am divine even as I live a human life." This was the realization that I came to which was so life changing: I and the Father are one. You are. *You and the Father are one.* Otherwise, you would not be. You would not be Life. You would not be living life. You would not have consciousness if you were not an extension of the Father.

When you realize that you are an *extension* of the Father, you come to the place of true joy, for you know that, truly, in that moment you are free, that your soul is free and that you do the work of the soul freely and joyously, and nothing else need be done except to take the deep breath and to abide in peace.

I and the Father are one. Know you how that changes your perspective on life itself? Know you what a sense of power it brings to you? Not power the way the world understands power, but power in the true sense of divinity that can never be threatened. It can never be at the mercy of the world; never at the mercy of time or others' decisions. *I and the Father are one.* You begin to realize then, "If I am here living this lifetime and I am one with the Father and I am all powerful, then I must have chosen to be here, because there is not a power outside of me that could or did send me here." In other words, you are not as some of the belief systems hold, that you have been relegated to a star system far, far out on the edges of the universe and forgotten somewhere. You have not been sent here to do penance for whatever. You are not here to work out your karma. You chose everything with free choice be-cause you wanted to know what it would feel like to experience it, and you wanted to come Home even through that experience.

When you realize that you chose to be here, then you begin to ask, as the master does in humbleness and humility—not as the world understands humility, but in true humility—"What am I here for? Why did I choose to be here?" To love, to serve, and to remember, individually and collectively. For if one of you catches the vision that *I and the Father are one,* it spreads to all of the collective consciousness as a yeast within the bread, and everything rises up. That is why you are here. You have chosen to live the life that seems to be not the master, and yet, it takes a master to choose to live the life that would deny its mastery.

It takes a master to choose to live a life that would appear not to be of mastery. Contemplate that when you put the head upon the pillow in this evening.

Now, having said that it takes a master to live a life which would seem to be not of mastery, many of you take that to the next step, and the conclusion is: "I must be a master, because my life does not look like it is being lived as a master." (Smile) Each one of you is a master who has chosen one more time to live a life, temporarily, in the cloak of forgetfulness; to serve the brothers and sisters who are a bit deeper into the dream of forgetfulness and to be as the yeast in the bread, to allow the rising up of the collective. *I and the Father are one.* That is the way of the master.

So be it.

Preparation for Ascension

Beloved one, shall we speak about ascension? It is a topic which has fascinated you lifetime after lifetime. It is a topic which you have contemplated, meditated upon, questioned, thought was something far removed from you, quite a miracle. You were present when I ascended the body, and you saw it to be quite a miracle in that day and time, which it was.

But ascension is not just assigned to an historical time long time ago. It is something truly that you can do, that you will do, that you have done. I say that you "have done," because as we speak of ascension there is a knowing deep within you, a relatedness you can understand, and if there is an understanding and a relatedness, it is because there is a program deep within you which remembers you have done it as well.

Take a moment, just a moment, to contemplate how it would feel to ascend the body in light. The body would be so light, radiant, that the law of gravity would no longer apply, and you would feel yourself light as the spirit, ascending the body. Can you visualize that? Can you feel that? Yes, for in truth, in what you would call another reality, you have already done it. Sometimes I hear you ask, "How can I ascend out of this world above my troubles? Would that I could be the spirit, free to fly above all of the troubles of the world."

In truth, in any moment you can ascend over the troubles whether you ascend the body or not. For verily I say unto you that the ascension of the body is not the end product. It is but a fringe benefit. What is important is the ascension in consciousness, to come up higher over everything which has seemed to weigh you down, to come up higher in consciousness to realize the oneness with spirit, with the Father, with the divine Isness which you are and always have been. That is the true ascension.

Whenever the voice of the world will present to you the questions, the confusion, the conflicts, allow yourself quickly to take the deep breath and to come unto the place of peace within the heart, there abiding in faith and in trust, asking for holy vision. It will be given to you and you will ascend over the problem, the conflict, the confusion.

Ascension, beloved one, is possible in every day: the ascension in consciousness. If it be part of your mission, your purpose, to make demonstration to ascend the body, then that will come as a result, a fringe benefit of the ascension in consciousness which you have been practicing moment by moment, day by day.

That is truly how my ascension happened. It was not by the touch of a magic wand and all of a sudden I went "poof." It was a process of remembrance, of *knowing* that I and the Father are one, the realization that I would not *be*—and this is true of you as well—if I were not life. I would not *be* if I were not one with the Father. I could have no being.

As I allowed myself to abide with that realization, walking every step of the journey knowing that I am one with the Father, there came such a remembrance that everything took on a new light.

Now, it is not necessary that you ascend the body in this lifetime or any other lifetime in order to be spiritual, in order to be loved of the Father, in order to graduate, in order to be of worth and value. It is not necessary as you would see a certain exam that you have to pass. You do not have to ascend the body.

For I say unto you, you do the most wonderful miracle in manifesting the body in the first place. Know you that the body is divine energy? It is light coalesced into form. Know you that that is a miracle, and you do it moment by moment? It would not stay together if you did not have the consciousness and a collective belief that there will be form coalesced out of light. So I say unto you that ascending the body is no more difficult and no more wonderful than what you do in manifesting the body. Think upon that for a bit.

After the resurrection I came and dwelt amongst you once again, and when I had shared with you many of the things which had been revealed to me, there came a knowing that it was time for me to absent myself physically. I knew that truly never could I be separate from you; always I carry you in my heart. So I gathered you and many others in our favorite gathering place and we sang with great joy. I spoke unto you of the oneness with the Father. I spoke to you, "Lo, I am with you always. It cannot be otherwise. You cannot go anywhere without me. I am with you always, even unto the end of the age." You have read this in your Scripture. However, there were a couple of words which were left out. They were understood at the time when the message was given, but they were not recorded. "Even unto the end of the age of forgetfulness." Lo, I am with you always, even unto the end of the age of forgetfulness, when, of course, you remember that I am one with you and we are one with the Father, and we are all one God Mind, and that is the end of the age of forgetfulness.

Being caught up in such an enlivenment, so caught up in the spirit of lightness, I allowed the body to return again to the Light which it is and ascended. This was called a miracle, and it was talked about, rumored about, and the word spread quickly.

Now, did I stay ascended? In other words, physically apart from you? No. I came, dwelt amongst you again, as I do even now sometimes when you are least expecting it.

What is important is to remember the true ascension, the ascension in consciousness, coming up higher with every realization that, "I and the Father are one. I am not held to this world. I am not bound by the world belief. I am the extension of the Father right here, right now." God so loved the world that he gave you to love it and to transform it, and in that realization you know your own ascension.

Now, how do you prepare for ascension, whether it be in consciousness—which, in truth, has to come first—or the physical ascension? It is to follow the way of the master. We have spoken of that already. The way of the master is to abide in peace. The way of the master is to abide as the beholder. The way of the master is to abide in trust.

Preparation for ascension is to know that truly you are one with the divine guidance. There is nothing outside of you. It is to know that you are the extension of the Father wherever you find yourself, and it is to abide in that place of divine Isness even while everything is whirling about you.

Preparation for ascension asks of you a discipline: a discipline of choice, of choosing the way of the master, the way of patience, asking whatever question, however complex it seems to be, to reveal its deeper meaning, its true meaning.

The way of the master is the way of love: loving all things; abiding with all things; allowing all things. The way of love looks past appearances and knows that everything works to bring forth the Christ.

Preparation for ascension is a discipline of choosing to live in joy, knowing that truly you are the joy of the Father come forth into expression. Preparation for ascension lies in appreciation, appreciating everything in your experience and finding joy in it.

When you abide with the discipline of the master, choosing to abide as the master, choosing to abide as the beholder, choosing to abide in love, choosing to abide in joy no matter what the circumstances be, choosing to claim and realize your freedom, your divinity, then you have known ascension.

Arise up, ascended one. Arise up and dance as the free spirit which you are. Arise up in joy, exultation. Arise up and know that you are the innocent one. You are ascended into a reality the world knows not. You are Home once again.

So be it.

The Meaning of Life

Now, in previous chapters we have spoken of the interdimensionality of you, the interdimensional Self which is beyond the self that you see as the individual you call yourself to be right now in this day and time. The interdimensional Self, the holy Self of you, is not focused upon a self as individuated energy, but is, in Truth, the true You. It is the matrix out of which you draw the creative energy to call yourself the individual with which you now identify.

We have spoken of this interdimensional You as being the most wonderful ocean of being. We have spoken of it as the

Mind of God, for it is truly the Isness, the consciousness of God, Allness, the creative Source. What you do in every moment is a great miracle: to bring the focus of attention so completely to an individual expression of the Allness of you that temporarily you put aside the remembrance of the Totality of you. It is a miracle that you do in every moment to call yourself an individuated self, and you do it for the most wonderful reasons. You do it for the adventure of the creative You, to see what you can experience and what you can express and what you can change momently.

I would speak to you now of worlds within worlds and dimensions within dimensions, and dimensions where there are not boundaries, limitations. Where you have placed your focus right now in this day and time is within a concept of the sphere of time, and it is truly that: it is a sphere and a concept of time where you see things to be linear, and yet all time is now. All time is now; all time is within the sphere of the concept of time.

You think back in history or even back in this lifetime to a point where something happened, and you see yourself to be at another point. What connects those two points is the straight line, and you take from that the truth—small "t"—of linear time. You project yourself into the future. You watch a science fiction movie, perhaps, of something that will be of the future, or you read articles of what is going to be in the future. You see yourself at this point, and you see yourself and the events at another point in time and you say, "That is the future. There is a line to that future, and I'm living a progression, a linear progression of experience."

Now, at the same time within the sphere of time you are living all of the other points as well, and as you will want to connect with other lifetimes, other expressions of yourself in what you would see to be past or future, you can do that, because there is no separation. You can go into what you see to be the past lifetimes and call forth the qualities, experiences, roles that you have had in those lifetimes and bring them forth into this now reality to serve you as experience to deal with whatever you are going through now.

You can do the same with going into the future, for the future is now. You are making your future even now as you sit here contemplating what the future can be, might be, should be, will be, you hope it might be, etc. You are making your future even as we speak, because you are playing with ideas, perceptions, limitations, and you are pushing out the limitations of what has been accepted by you and by the collective consciousness for so long.

There are many expressions within the Mind of God. There are many expressions and experiences of the holy Self of you. This is but one of them, even as you would see everything that is contained within this point of time— and this is but one point of focus within the sphere of time— and I will say to you that this sphere of consciousness and the concept of time is but one reality. It is as you would see the drop of water in the vast ocean.

There are many, many realities where you know unlimitedness, where you flow as liquid crystal and you have consciousness of being. It is not that you go into a nothingness or an unknowing; you have consciousness of being, and yet you know yourself to be unlimited. You know yourself to be light, laughter, expanded joy. You do not know yourself to be constricted by time or by years or by the certain aging of the body. There are many experiences within the Mind of God, the interdimensional Self of you, which do not have form as you know form to be. Consciousness, yes. Awareness, yes. Isness, yes. Intelligence, yes, even vaster—and I do not mean to put you down—but even vaster than the intelligence that you claim now in this point of consciousness.

You are much greater than the point of focus which you claim in this point of time. You are outside of time, and yet you are within time. You are outside of space, and yet you are within space and taking up space, as you understand physical laws. You are beyond any restrictions of expression, even though the body will speak to you of certain limitation. You are beyond that, and that is where the rub comes in from time to time, because you know yourself to be beyond what the body tells you, beyond what the body would suggest is the truth of your being. You are beyond that, and the rub comes in when the body dictates to you certain limitations and you know those limitations not to be true, and yet how do you overcome the collective consciousness that believes so strongly in the physical form? Gradually. That is how you are doing it. You have decreed that it will be an evolution of consciousness, but you have also decreed that you are going to accelerate the process to get to the place where you know the holy Self of you.

You are pushing out the boundaries of the collective consciousness, but you have built in a safety measure within this reality, the concept of time, where you have said that there is going to be process. There is going to be time to think about consequences. Yet at the same time you get impatient with the process, because you do remember instant manifestation, and you do know that, in Truth, it does not take time to manifest. It can be in an instant. But I say to you that there is value in process. It is a safety measure, and it works very well. It gives you opportunity for reflection before you manifest.

Now, outside of time, imagine for a moment yourself as a flow of liquid crystal. Imagine a crystal being heated, even in physical terms, to the place where it becomes liquid and it flows with a consciousness of being, without perhaps a goal as to where it is going to flow. It is just an Isness of flow, or a consciousness within light—let us call it that, if you want—an Intelligence, and it is flowing. It does not have to have a goal in mind. Goal often is time-oriented, within the concept of time. But you are Light, Intelligence, experiencing and expressing, unlimited, just for the sheer joy of being, just to know yourself as Being, totally outside of any restrictions, living in the Mind of God, expressing as the Mind of God, and looking into the most wonderful concept of time to see what is happening there, as you would within a crystal ball perhaps, to see what is going on, and to choose once in awhile to come and be part of it; or to look within other concepts of dimensions and realities that are yet concepts and to see what is happening within those concepts, and to see if you want to be part of that concept, that reality, or not; to do as you do with your television set, to flip through the channels to see what's on, just to see what is playing now. You look up your movie theaters to see what is playing now at the movies. The holy Self of you does that: looks in on you. The greater Self of you watches to see, "What drama is she into now? What drama is he making for himself now? What peace is she finding, mellowness? What solutions, what questions, what interrelationships are happening?"

In other realities that are not within the concept of time there are interrelationships as well, and there is a knowing of certain coming together in the flow, a sharing, a mind melding, if you will, and then an agreement to go again separate ways, although not separate at all.

What I am doing with you in this time right now is teasing the mind to bring you to a point where you understand the concept of this reality of time and see it as but one concept, a most beautiful concept, within that which is greater and is truly conceptless, although it contains the concepts of different realities. It is difficult within a finite concept to explain that which is infinite and beyond concept, but I am teasing you with it so that you play with, "Perhaps it does not matter so much what the body tells me, what the world tells me. Perhaps I do not live in the world, but the world lives in me. I am not at the mercy of the world, of the body, of others' decisions. I am not vulnerable, cannot be threatened by anything that seems to come in the appearance as threatening or upsetting or leading to insecurity. The holy Self of you cannot be threatened. It does not even understand the concept of being threatened. The holy Self of you is forever ongoing.

The meaning of life is expansiveness. Your scientists are now discovering that your universe is expanding. They are proving it by what they see in the most wonderful technology of your telescopes, the ones that are situated here on our holy Mother, the Earth, this planet, and the ones that are out in space, traveling to get a different perspective and to bring to the remembrance of ones here the light which has been, so that there is an understanding of what has been in the beginning, as they call it.

The meaning of life is expansiveness. It is to be forever ongoing, even within the concept of time. You are ones who, because of what we have been speaking of right now, are bursting the bubble of the concept of time, and you walk outside of that bubble for a moment or so—which is still a bit of a contradiction to use that terminology, but for a moment or so you walk outside of the concept of time—and you see yourself to be in the infinite flow of Isness which is forever ongoing.

The meaning of life is to go for it, to live it. *I am come that they might have life, and that they might have it more abundantly;* in other words, to know truly Who you are and to live from the place of the holy Self. *I and the Father are one.* I am the Father in expression. I am Life eternal, even beyond the eternality which is still in the concept of time. I Am That Which I Am, not circumscribed by any concept or restriction.

Life is expansive. That is why you get ideas to do things. That is why after you sit on your duff for a short time, you want to be up and doing. That is why you are forever imagining what you can do, where you can go, who you can talk to, ideas you can play with, projects that you want to accomplish. Life is expansion. Even after you release the body, the expansion does not stop. In truth, you expand even further, because you are not restricted by the belief of what the body has been telling you the physicality has to be according to all of the physical laws that you as a collective have agreed to. You go beyond the body. You go beyond a certain point, a most wonderful point, into the infinite awareness of the Allness of you. Then you make choice, if you want to, to step back into the concept of time in another reality within time or not. You may choose.

Many of you have said, "This is the last lifetime I am going to have on this plane. I am going to complete everything in this lifetime so I don't have to come back here again." Well, I have news for you. You never have to come back here. It is always a choice, but oftentimes you will choose to come back because you are curious. You want to know, "How expansive can I be within the constrictions of the collective consciousness?" That is what you have been doing in this lifetime. "How expansive can I be within the boundaries which the collective consciousness has put up as truth?"—small "t".

You have found yourself to be the iconoclasts, the ones who are always going beyond the boundaries, who are always seeking for something more, something different, always wanting to know. "There has to be more. I know there is more than just this concept of time, wonderful as it is. There is more to me, and I want to connect with it once again and do a most miraculous thing. I want to bring that awareness even into the confines of the sphere of time and the limited reality." See you how great you are as masters—which you are—that you would even dare to think such a thought? But you have done it over and over. It is a role which you know very well, because you have played it many times, where you have looked in on a reality and you have said, "Aha. I wouldn't mind going in there and maybe pushing out some boundaries, even if it makes the biological family a little upset with me, even if it makes the relationships question me. You know, I really wouldn't mind playing that part for awhile."

Then you come as the small child and you learn all of what the collective consciousness says has to be truth—small "t"—and you acquiesce for awhile to forget, and yet there is the inner Voice within you which prompts you to search, to seek, to know, to find that which feels like Home, and to be with other ones who recognize Home when they find it in you, as they find it in themselves. That is why you go to gatherings to find ones of like mind; you read the books, articles to find the spark of remembrance of Home.

When I spoke to you that the Father is love, it was to convey the idea of expansiveness, for as you are in love with another one or with a beloved pet, there is an expansiveness which happens within you. You feel your whole soul open up, as the flower will open to the sun. That expansiveness is Life itself. It is the meaning of Life. It is the meaning of You. It is your true nature. When the prophecies of doom and gloom and of closing down come to you, there is a reaction which you feel. There is a closing down even in the solar plexus of the body—well-named for the sun, for light—that does not feel good. It feels like constriction. So when ones speak to you of doom and gloom and a closing down, there is a great part of you that rises up and says, "This isn't true. I know it not to be true. I know that I have lived," and you have, "through many closing downs that were just concepts of closing down, and not True—capital 'T'." Dramas, yes; adventures, yes; and you played your parts very well, but not True—capital "T".

Life is expansive, even individual life as you have claimed this part of your beingness. It is expansive. That is why you get caught up with the new ideas. That is why you feel expansive when you contemplate going somewhere, doing something new. Yes, there may be a feeling of excitement and a feeling of questioning if you are going into new territory, a new job perhaps, or even a new dwelling place, a new location. There is a bit of excitement, and that excitement truly is the expansiveness of you. It is bringing in the holy energy of the Creator.

Long enough now you have acquiesced to what the world said had to be, all of the drama of the world. You have seen much of the drama and you know that it repeats itself over and over, and it will continue within the concept of time and the reality of linear time as it is seen. There will be a repeating and a repeating and a repeating and a repeating until ones such as you burst the bubble of time itself, and you move outside of it to be the beholder of what is going on within the concept of time, even this point, right here within the sphere of time, and you even move outside of the sphere long enough to say,

"Hey, you know, look at all of those galaxies that are acknowledged to be within that reality of time. Look what they're
doing. They're expanding. What's that going to do with the
concept of time?"

It is going to make for change, an expansiveness, if you
will. The meaning of Life is expansiveness, creativity. Do that
which you have been desiring to do. Allow the concept of time
to be played with in your meditation, in your musing, in times
when you are doing the daily activities that do not require
much of the mind to do and you find your mind wandering off
onto other ideas. Play with, "What could be outside the concept of time; not only just this point of time, but all of time?
My god, if there is something outside of that, what is it?" And
you will find yourself, your true Self, in that expansiveness,
and you will feel and you will know truly that Life is not the
body. The body serves you well, yes, for a point of focus in a
lifetime. But the body is not Who you are. Life is Who you
are. The expansiveness, the ongoingness of life is Who you
are, and the ideas, the consciousness of ideas that you play
with, are part of the creativity of the wholeness of you. That is
Life itself, and it does not have to be, *is not*, circumscribed,
constrained by physicality.

Now, I am not saying to you in these words that you should
decease the body. That is not what I am saying, because the
body is most wonderful, and you have chosen it so that you
can walk through this lifetime in relationship with others, and
so that you can have the physical pleasure of the body. I am
not saying to you to decease the body so that you can get
outside the concept of time. What I am saying to you is that
Life itself is more than the body. Life itself is the expansiveness of creative Isness, and you live that Life irrespective of
the physical laws. And that, beloved one, is freeing. That free
perspective is where I live and did live, even on the cross, to

the place of the deceasement of the body. I was still alive, even with the deceasement of the body. Understand you that point? Good.

Life, the meaning of Life, is expansiveness, ongoingness, creativity. When you allow yourself to move into the place of the beholder, to step outside of time just for a moment or so, when you allow yourself to move into the consciousness of the interdimensional Self which is not constricted by any dimension, any reality, you begin to get the flavor of how infinite, powerful, creative you are. I have spoken many times with you about how you are an extension of the Father, come into this plane of reality. I spoke with you in terms which could be understood as a child of the Father, a beloved child of the Father, which in Truth you are. Then there came the concept that you were co-creators of the reality you experience. Then we took it one step further to the place where I am impressing upon you that you are an *extension*, not just a co-creator, not just a child as you would see an offspring to be, but an *extension* of the Father, creative One, come into this point of reality to live the human life from a divine point of view. You knew this as little children when you ran around innocent and free for at least a moment or so before all of society and the parents clapped upon you the "shoulds" and "shouldn'ts."

So where does this take you? It takes you to the place of the Allness of you, before and beyond time. It takes you to the Mind of God. It takes you to your true Self, your holy Self. You live the human life, yes, but you live it from a divine perspective. That is what you have agreed you will do. You will suffer the slings and arrows of the world and you will allow them to bounce off of you, because truly the holy Self cannot be threatened, cannot be harmed. The holy Self of you is outside time, before and beyond.

The Meaning of Life

I have often said to you that when the purpose of time has been fulfilled--in other words, when ones have played with the concept of time to the place of saying, "I know that now, inside and out, intimately, every point within it; I am satisfied, satiated, completed with it"--then the expanding galaxies will have expanded into the Allness which is you, within the Mind of God, which is you.

So I thank you for what you are doing in this day and time, because you are allowing the individual mind—lower case "m"—to play with the possibility, probability, and reality of the Mind—capital "M"—of you, of God; You as God. For eons of time, as you understand linear time to be, you have revered a God somewhere outside of you, and you have said that this God is all-powerful, and It is. But you have forgotten that you are not separate from this God which you revere. As you have lived a lifetime, you have been the point of consciousness of the Mind of God, as Life itself, each lifetime. So even though you would deny that which you are in every lifetime, and you would have said, "But God is out there somewhere, all-powerful, and I am down here somewhere, separate," you in that lifetime, as expression of Life, were, have been, will be, and are the Mind of God in expression.

With that thought in mind, I will allow you to contemplate it, to live in expansiveness, to give the encouragement to ones, to live as the Light which you are, and to know that Life truly is expansive; it does not end with the deceasement of the body; it does not begin with the picking up of a body, but is forever ongoing. Life is what you make of it. It is expansive. Whether you deny it or whether you accept it, it is expansive. Go with that thought in mind and live it truly.

So be it.

Moving Into Fifth Dimensional Consciousness

Beloved one, there has been much energy shifting in the recent past, and I would speak with you now of energy shift, of enlightenment, of preparation and moving into a new dimension, that which you call the 5th dimension. For truly, many of you will be moving into 5th dimensional expression and experience.

In the beginning before time was, the vast ocean of the Mind of God is, was, will be forever, You. The Mind of God, being expansive as it is, desired to be dynamic, forever creating. You, as the gods which you are, asked of yourself and each other as there became a knowing of individuated energy, "What can we create? What would be fun to experience? What kind of script can we write?" You are still writing and expanding on those scripts. You conceived of many, many realities—lower case "r"—in order to expand on the knowingness of You—capital "Y".

One of the realities that you fashioned is *this* reality in which you now play. You have played in this reality many lifetimes over and over, and you have gotten it down pretty well so that you know many of the answers; not all of them, because you have said, "I don't want to know all of the answers just yet. I want it to be a process of discovery." So it becomes a process of discovery, and as you are doing the discovery you also build into it the most wonderful gift of improv, so that what you have thought you might discover, in the next moment you do some improv and it is something else that you discover about yourself and what you can create.

You are beginning collectively to value the diversity of expression. It is a place now where your scripting is undergoing such a wonderful improv that, in truth, there cannot be the prophecies of what is going to be as a definite prophecy. There can be, as it is seen now, the possibility and even the probability of certain trends, but you are so much coming into your claiming of the divinity of you and the expressive quality of the Christ nature that ones cannot write what has not yet been written, and that is a very exciting place to be.

However, from the greater Mind of you—capital "M"-you can see trends and possibilities, probabilities. You are moving, as it is seen now, into a most wonderful place of beginning to understand Oneness, to value diversity and yet to see Oneness through the diversity, much as you see the various facets of the gemstone. The gemstone itself is one stone, and yet it has many facets that reflect the brilliance.

You are the One expressing as the many. Everything that you contemplate, that you meditate upon, that you dream, hope for, is felt and registered within the collective. Nothing is ever done in isolation, even though bodies speak of separation, even though you say, "Well, I am here and you are there, and I have certain personality and you have certain personality traits, and we are separate one from another." It is only on a certain level that separation is seen, and beyond that there is the great pool of Mind from which you draw ideas, even feelings and emotions.

You are moving now into 5th dimension where you know oneness with others. You know what they are thinking. There is a resonance within you. You can feel what others are feeling. You are becoming more and more aware, sensitive to energy patterns and to dimensional vibration as well.

In the beginning of this reality when you thought to have process, to have time, we brought forth the most wonderful creations upon the Earth, and we knew ourselves to be one with the energy of our holy Mother, the Earth. Nowadays many take for granted what they walk upon. They are not aware that it is holy ground you walk upon anywhere on the Earth, and yet it is vibrational life, a different vibration than what you have made your body so that there can be a support. In other words, when you step on our holy Mother, the Earth, there is a vibrational quality that does not allow you to just go right straight through it. You have planned and created well.

In the beginning when we played upon the Earth, the Light which we are danced upon the firmament. We brought forth terra firma. You have that phrase in your vocabulary even in this day and time. We brought forth, as the Light which we were, the energy of Christ to play upon that which we were creating, and we knew ourselves to be Light, and we went with Light flowing, creating. Various ones joined in vibratory resonance with others as to what you would call now in your parlance, committees, to bring forth various forms of life, large and small: trees, flowers, mountains, valleys, rivers, waterfalls.

After a process of time there was a temporary setting aside of the remembrance of Who/What created the creation, and you brought forth out of this temporary forgetting the 1st dimension, as you would look upon it now. Now, what we speak of are concepts, not the Reality of you—capital "R"—but concepts that you as the creative one have brought forth in this reality—lower case "r"—to play with. You brought forth 1st dimension. You did not call it that, because at that point there was not any thought of dimensions. It was just existence, just to be, in what you would see now looking back through linear history the ancient times of the caveman, the dinosaurs, pre-history of just existence—1st dimensional.

Then there was, as there is with creative process, an evolution, an expansion if you will, into, "How do I defend what I think I am and what I have created?" You came into what is now in your concept of linear development, 2nd dimension, where there was a feeling of isolation. Now, 1st dimension did not know isolation. First dimension only knows existence. The 2nd dimension knew an awareness of the existence of different vibrations, which led to a belief in the need to protect, defend; a dimension where ones existed, and much of the energy was used to exist and to protect what little one seemed to have. There was not much of an expansion; there was some, but not much of even thought or awareness of expansion or what else might be. There was the underlying belief in isolation and a feeling of, "I must defend," because other ones would come together in groups as the marauders who would overrun a geographical area that was not even organized into a political gathering—settlements, I suppose you would call them. There was always the nagging fear that, "What little I have may be taken from me." That was 2nd dimension.

Then you have moved in the collective evolution into a more expanded 3rd dimension where most of your reality is yet rooted in the feeling of isolation, the feeling of separation, the feeling of warring vibrational energy, a feeling of need for more complex protection, and you have seen now your technology developing to the place where, "I can protect myself and my loved ones against whatever, and even if I have to use outer space, I will use that as means of the technology to defend that which I feel I have to defend." You have become very adept, as a collective, in protecting that which you are now creating more and more.

There is great complexity of abundance of things, material things, of families, of dwelling places, of technology. You have the complexities of various groupings that play games to protect. Much as you see the chess game, there are ones in 3rd dimensional reality who find drama in playing the chess game of how to move various pieces—in other words, the armies and the troops—into various positions. It is seen by some of these ones who are directing it as a chess game, with no feeling of oneness or identification with the chess pieces they are setting into various positions.

Yet there are many of you who are moving beyond 3rd dimension because there is a remembrance, the still small Voice within, which speaks of something better. Quite often there has been the feeling of, "I don't know exactly what it is, but I know that there has to be something more than just defending. There has to be something more than just fear which wreaks havoc upon the body and in the affairs. There has to be something more." And you begin to hope.

Hope is one of the greatest gifts that you have brought into the scripting, where you know from some long time ago that there must have been something better. You begin to draw to yourself teachers who will speak to you of that which has been before this reality which believes so much in isolation and in the need for defense. You bring to yourself the books, the recordings that speak to the very soul of you to nurture that soul as it would a small bud of a flower and to allow it to begin to open, to bloom. That is what is happening now as you are moving from 3rd dimension into 4th and then into 5th.

There will be many of you who will move easily into 5th dimension, not releasing the body, not releasing the knowing of what it means to live in 3rd dimension, and yet being able to go back and forth at will, to activate the body and yet know 5th dimensional Oneness, Love, Compassion, and to behold the most divine dance of the collective, the evolution of the collective.

Now, as we speak of that, there is a certain resonance, a certain knowing, for many of you have lived the monastic life in other lifetimes where you denied the world because it was too heavy. It was too complex. It was too conflicted. You denied the world and you lived the monastic life in 5th dimensional awareness. That is why, even in this lifetime, there are times when you want to take yourself apart from the maddening crowd and go away to be in peace, in solitude. It is because you remember the lifetimes you have spent where you were in 5th dimensional awareness. You were still in 3rd dimensional reality, but you said, "I will not deal with it." You built physical walls around the monasteries to keep the villagers and the riffraff outside so they could do their drama out there, but you did not have to behold it.

This lifetime you have said from a place of great courage, "I am going to be part of all of the drama; I am going to know it intimately to the place of completion, and I am going to move into the place of beholder, the place of 5th dimensional awareness, and I am going to speed up the evolution of the collective consciousness." That is your purpose. That is why you are here: you are speeding up the evolution of collective consciousness.

Now, you are very good in this reality in putting everything into categories and levels. It helps you to understand, and the concepts are very good as stepping stones. However, what we speak of is more awareness than dimension, and you are moving already into an evolutionary leap of collective consciousness. You already are on the cusp, if you will, of moving through 4th into 5th.

Now you ask, "Well, what is 4th dimension?" Fourth dimensional awareness happens when you are in a meditative state. It is a place you go when you want to have expanded understanding. It is not separate from 3rd dimensional awareness, but it is an expansion of it as you move from 3rd dimension into 4th with your intuition, meditation, contemplation, musing.

In 4th dimensional consciousness in what is called imagination or in meditation, you bring forth information which allows you then to move into 5th dimension. Fifth dimensional awareness is where you know Who you are. You realize, "I am the Christ incarnate. I am Life itself." It is not heresy to say, "I am the Christ," because you are, truly. It is the Christ energy which allows you to activate the body. It is Life itself—capital "L"—that allows you to live the life—lower case "l"—that you call your reality and to play your drama.

In 5th dimensional awareness you know, "I am a master, playing the game from time to time of thinking that I am not a master. I am the master who is so creative and so powerful that I can play temporarily in a place where I deny my power, where I can say that I am the victim of others' decisions or of what the body tells me."

Fifth dimensional consciousness is unconditional, unlimited love and a knowing of Oneness, a knowing of Who you are, the great master who has chosen once again to come into a 3rd dimensional reality or 2nd or 1st, as you have done, and to accept temporarily the scripting of that dimension, and yet to move the collective consciousness in the evolutionary process through those dimensional awarenesses to the place where you know the master which you are, and you can come and go and function in 3rd dimensional reality knowing, as you have known many times, this is not your true being.

However, as you are moving in 5th dimensional consciousness, it will not deny 3rd dimensional, and it will not deny 4th dimensional, where you have the intuition and the knowing of the energy which is going on. It will not deny that which others accept yet for awhile to be the reality—lower case "r"—but it means that you will stand in the place of the master and you will choose, consciously choose.

Now, 3rd dimensional awareness has scripted that there is not conscious choice about the big things. There is conscious choice about, perhaps, the raiment that you are going to put on, or there is conscious choice about what you are going to eat, at least in 3rd dimension—sometimes in 1st or in 2nd there was not even that choice—but 3rd dimensional has said, "You get choice over the small things, but over the big things, forget it. There is somebody else outside there, up there, who is calling all of the shots." When you allow yourself 5th dimensional consciousness, you recognize that you choose in every moment that which you are going to express and that which you are going to experience. It is a conscious choice in 5th dimensional consciousness to live as the master who has temporarily taken upon his/her shoulders the cloak of forgetfulness.

As you go in 5th dimensional consciousness, you are very much aware of brothers and sisters and where they are coming from. You see everything and everyone as they truly are. You will see, yes, the appearance that they present to you, the 3rd dimensional reality that they believe in, but you will see more than that. You will see Who they truly are. You will see the Christ energy at work, even in the games that they want to play.

Our holy Mother, the Earth, is also feeling an evolutionary leap into new dimensional vibration. There is a vibratory quality of light which is infusing the Earth, much the same as when we have spoken about the golden white light, the aura around the body, which is the Christ energy activating the body.

There is an aura about our holy Mother, the Earth, which extends many, many miles farther out into space. There is much that is being activated to speed up that which you feel in your consciousness and in your physicality, and there is much that is being activated upon and within the Earth, because She is not separate from you and you are not separate from Her. There is a consciousness within Her that is also evolving, that is also moving towards the place of 5th dimensional awareness. There is a consciousness arising to the place where you will know communication with ones who stand ready now to help with the evolutionary shift. They are available in certain areas and will make themselves known unto you as there is willingness for ones to receive.

I would do with you again what is called the meditation. Allow yourself to take the deep breath and to feel the peace which descends with the deep breath. Allow yourself to contemplate the inner earth, the central sun, for truly there is a sun within our holy Mother, the Earth. Contemplate the light of that sun within the Earth. Feel the color, the vibration, what it would be like. In that contemplation feel an Intelligence which surrounds everything, every created thing, an Intelligence which surrounds and is infused in everything. Feel the consciousness of the central sun. Do not worry about the physical body and how it would be in the heat. Just feel the consciousness as your mind takes you there. And in that consciousness of the central sun, allow yourself to acknowledge that there are, as you yet understand it, beings of intelligence that express Mind—capital "M"—of All That Is.

There is a wisdom that has been planted there from the beginning of time, from the beginning of creation. There is a wisdom there which will abide beyond the purpose of time. Know that this wisdom is not separate from you. It is part of your wisdom as you now meet it mind to mind.

Allow out of that central sun, and out of that Intelligence, a form to come towards you, a form of a master, perhaps, as you would understand a master to be. That form comes towards you with hands outstretched. That form comes towards you in radiance, in love, in welcoming, and in an invitation of wanting to be welcomed. See yourself walking towards this form with your hands stretched out to join, to meet in a place of love, a place of harmony and acceptance, the place that says,

"I know you from before time began." As you join hands, allow yourself to walk to a place of shelter, a place to sit, facing each other, and speak to each other that which the heart wants to speak. Ask the questions you would ask of a master: cosmic questions, general questions, personal questions, anything that comes to mind that you would ask of a master. Then listen.... Allow the master to speak to you the answer to what you would ask. Then allow the master to ask his or her question of you; for indeed, they come with questions as well. Listen to his or her question. What would they ask of cosmic nature, general nature, even personal nature? Then respond as you understand. Feel the shared commonality of oneness. Allow your heart to open, to receive that which they will give to you. Allow your heart to open to give to them that which they ask.

When you have conversed with each other to the place where there is a feeling of completeness, agree to meet again, for any time you want to speak with this one, they will come, and any time they will invite you, there will be a knock upon the door of your mind to open and to talk. For, in truth, there is no separation. When you have agreed to meet again, allow yourselves to stand, hands still joined, and to smile with a radiance one upon the other, and slowly take leave of each other, the form receding back into the central sun, and you coming back to what you call yourself.

And now, taking another deep breath, allow the consciousness to come back to the body that you claim to be your own. Taking another deep breath to energize the body and the consciousness of this reality, bring with you the peace, the understanding, the intelligence, the communion, if you will, that you have had in these short moments, and know that truly you have moved from 3rd dimension through 4th into 5th. Keep with you the blessing of this peace, for never do you walk alone. Even in the times when you have put yourself in the box and you have said, "I am alone; this is all there is, and it is not enough," even at those times the Intelligence of you—capital "I"—has walked with you, has seen you through, has guided, encouraged, and worked what you would call the miracles, and the miracles are yet to continue.

So be it.

The Beholder Activist

We have been speaking the last few times of realities, of dimensions, what you make for yourself as the sandboxes to play in. We have been speaking how this reality—small "r"—is but one of the sandboxes that you make to play in. It is one where you build the sandcastles, and then when you have built as much as you want of the sandcastle you have choice to knock it over and to build another one of different design for the fun of it, just for the creative fun of it.

We have been speaking of how you have made for yourself concepts and boxes within this reality, boxes with labels, where you have felt as a collective consciousness there was a certainty, a security within that box, and yet at the same time you wanted to push out the sides of the box because you felt that there must be something more.

We spoke of the different dimensional perspectives that you have had through eons of time, with 1st dimensional consciousness being just that of existence, of having the physical body, the vehicle to express within the physical laws which you have collectively designed and agreed upon, just of keeping the body alive, whatever form of body it was. In what you would see as linear time, in the earliest of times the bodies were not the humanoid that you know now, but they were different forms, because you wanted to play with different forms to see what it would feel like to have the very large or small form or to feel what it would be like to swim in the ocean or to fly. You experimented with different forms.

You have your mythology which has come down to you of the half-human and half-animal and you have said, "Well, that couldn't be. How could that ever...that wouldn't be. Animals are beneath humans, so how would there ever be form where there would be half-human and half-animal?" And yet you played with those forms because you wanted to know, "How would it feel?" The mythology speaks to you of Truth—capital "T"—of the creative nature of you. Animals are not beneath you. Animals are a living form; no matter what the form is, there is a divine spark of spirit which activates that form.

You played with 1st dimensional perspective and came unto a certain evolution over what you would see to be a very long time, and yet as you would measure it against all of eternity, it is as a snap of the fingers.

You came to 2nd dimensional perspective by a gradual evolution. It was a gradual change in perspective to the place where there was a bit more of the gathering of humans together and a tending, if you will, of the other forms of life. You have in your Scriptures, because it was written as the thinking of that day, where God gave man—and woman—dominion over the animals of the field. Well, that was the thinking of that time.

Second dimensional perspective had to do with existence yet, but a little bit more of the collective grouping together and what could be done as a group. The consciousness evolved, again with a little more of the complexity of groupings, realizing that the group depended on each other working together as one village, tribe, grouping. Yet because there was the belief in separation, there was the feeling that a village, a tribe had to be defended against another group that might appear on the horizon.

Then there was evolution of perspective bringing you into 3rd dimensional perspective, which is where most of the collective consciousness has been for some time now as you measure, again, the linear time. Third dimensional perspective has much more complexity to it. There is still the belief in separation. There is still the belief in the necessity for preservation of the physical vehicle, the body. But you have taken it to a place where there is much more of the complexity, where you can try to do manipulation for your own defense at what would be a safe distance; where you have played with the manipulations of power. This also was known in 2nd dimensional perspective as it evolved into 3rd. There was much of the manipulation of temporal power. Third dimensional thinking has much to do, again, with separation, the need for defense or offense, and the manipulation of worldly power.

But you are coming now to a place where you have been
seeing that that sandcastle and that sandbox does not satisfy. It
can be quite beautiful. Some of the times you have been the
leaders, the kings, the queens, the ones who wielded much
power, seemingly, over others; where you have been the presi-
dents or prime ministers or whatever the labeling would be of
the grouping; where you had vast troops at your disposal who
could do your bidding, and you sat safely somewhere at a
distance. You have seen that that did not fulfill and did not
answer the very deep question within you as to the purpose of
life. There must be something more. The still small Voice is
always asking, always motivating.

So you have looked at that sandcastle from all sides. You
have been the kings, the queens, the prime ministers, the ones
who ruled. You have been the ones who *were* ruled, the ones
who were as the troops, the ones who were the servants, the
ones who did the bidding of others who seemingly had more
power. You played your scripts very well, with all of the
nuances, over and over, until you have come to a place where
you have said, "I'm complete with that sandcastle. I know
what it looks like from the outside. I know what it looks like
from the inside. I know what it looks like from the perspective
of looking down at it. I am finished with that one. I want to
know, truly, what is *sand*?"

You come to a very basic question. That is where collective
consciousness is now in its evolution: standing upon the
threshold of completion with a certain sandcastle. You see
much of conflict. It is brought to you on your airwaves, your
television, your news media, your papers, even on the world-
wide web. There is information that comes to you of conflict
and completion. Count it all as good. Even though it does not
look to be good, it is working to bring ones who are involved
in whatever is going on to the place where they are finished

with that sandcastle. They are going to say, "Okay, I have built everything out of the sand in this sandbox, and there must be a greater purpose than just building sandcastles."

You are moving now into a place of 4th dimensional perspective. You call upon that, truly, in every day. That is where you ask for the holy vision. That is where you ask to see the greater picture of what is going on, where you have intuition which tells you that there is much more than just what the news media brings you, the little blurb of two or three sentences that they give you about happenings. You wonder, "What is behind that? What is the motivation? The ones who were doing whatever the event was, what was their motivation? What were they like as children? How were they molded in their growing-up years?" Even if you see them as the teen-aged ones who are taking up arms and behaving as though they would be the grey beards, "What was their molding and how did they start out? Why do they see it necessary to do whatever choices they are doing?"

So you ask those questions in 4th dimensional questioning and you wait for an answer. The answer comes through in the quiet times, perhaps as you are going about your daily activity of driving the vehicle, washing the dishes, taking the shower, whatever. The answer comes to you that there must be much more that is happening here.

You move into a place of 5th dimensional perspective where you do, indeed, have the holy vision; where you do, indeed, see that threads, seemingly separate, are being woven together into a beautiful tapestry, into a beautiful place of the completion where ones will lay down the swords, where ones will lay down all of the great and grandiose plans for ruling and will say, "You are my sister, you are my brother. Surely we can live together in harmony. There must be a way, because we have tried all of the other sandcastles and they have not brought us fulfillment." You sometimes stay in 5th dimensional consciousness for a moment or so, sometimes for a bit longer as to the length of the meditation, as to the length of what you are willing to contemplate. You get a glimpse of something much larger than just 3rd dimensional density, separation, need for defense, invulnerability. You come to the place where you realize that, "The Spirit which I am cannot be threatened. The body, yes, can be asked of me and I can release it, but the Spirit of me cannot be threatened. It is from before time, and it will continue after the purpose of time has been completed. It will continue in its expansion to create, to experience, to express."

The realization brings you to a certain place of peace within, that no matter what else is going on around you—and there may be much of chaos going on around you— the Spirit of you needs no defense. The Spirit of you has always been and will forever be. That gives you pause to breathe, to breathe the divine breath of the connection with your oneness with the Father, Mother, God, Goddess, All That Is. It gives to you new perspective as to what you have to do with 3rd dimensional activities.

You are at a most wonderful place now where you are bridging 3rd dimensional perspective, because you understand world perspective, you know what the brothers and sisters are feeling. You have been there. You have felt it yourself, and there are many times when you cry unto the heavens and you would like something changed. Then you take that deep breath and you bridge to the 5th dimension for a moment or so, into the divine peace of Allness.

You are doing much that helps in the evolution of the collective consciousness. As an entity, the collective consciousness has a soul, and that soul is crying out for healing, the same as individual souls are crying out for healing. The collective consciousness is at a place now where it is ready to entertain a new perspective. Those of you who are willing, as you are, to be complete with the old sandcastles and to move on to the bigger questions as to "What is sand, what is this box I think I am in; perhaps it isn't a box after all; I thought it was a sandbox, but where are the boundaries, where are the edges?," as you are willing to play with these questions, you affect all of collective consciousness, because *there is no separation*. What you do goes out and touches other ones. You have seen this as you have been with a friend who has been struggling with a problem and they have asked you for help. You may not know the specific answer to whatever their problem is, but you have known that there is an answer, and sometimes when ones are so close up against a problem, they cannot see that there even would be an answer. They feel like everything is coming down on top of them and there is no way out, no hope.

You sit with them and you say, "Well, I don't know exactly what the answer is, but I know there is an answer. I know that it is not quite as dark and as heavy as you have perceived it to be." With that small mustard seed of hope you have changed the vibration that the other one was in. With that small bit of new perspective, a shift, and it *is* a shift, you have given to them a vibrational upliftment. It gives them a new vibrational quality which then moves them into a space where they can entertain ideas of change.

As you are abiding as the bridge between 3rd dimensional thinking which you know so well and 5th dimensional freedom, you find yourself more and more in the place of beholder, the place where you can see and understand what 3rd dimension is all about. You know it very well. You have played the scripting over and over and over and over, and when you were not actively playing the script, you were in the wings waiting for the next time you would be on the stage.

So you know 3rd dimensional thinking very well, but you are now spending more and more of your time in 5th dimensional perspective in a place that knows hope, that knows holy vision, and you see with greater clarity how everything works together to bring out the divinity which has been forgotten for so long. As you are in the place of beholder, ideas come to you which you then bring back and put into action in 3rd dimensional perspective because you have a wider vision, a greater understanding of how things fit together. You become the Beholder Activist—which sounds like a contradiction, and yet it is not—because you come from the place of beholder where you ask for the holy vision, and then you bring the ideas from that place and put them into action in 3rd dimension, as in giving to another one the words of advice, encouragement, as in rising up and speaking your truth.

In the months to come there will be many actors playing the scripts upon the stage. You will envision from 5th dimensional perspective that which you know can be, which will allow you to speak your truth and to be the activist in 3rd dimension, to come together with others of like mind and to speak out for what you believe and what you know can be, and for what you know *will* be, because there *will* be evolution of consciousness; that is a given. The timing of it is up to the improv. That is up to the one-hundredth monkey concept, where all of a sudden there is a shift that does happen in the evolution because enough of the collective consciousness has gotten it.

With your perspective from 5th dimension, from holy vision, from the place that knows divine clarity, you work in 3rd dimension. That is why, truly, you have taken incarnation at this time: to be the Beholder Activist, to bring a new perspective to this place which is crying out for the evolutionary leap. The harvest is ready. It has seemed in times past that the harvest was aplenty, but the harvesters were few, but you are meeting more and more ones who are ready to help with the harvesting, the evolution of collective consciousness into a new perspective. You have agreed that you will come together once again and you will write on your web, you will write on your papyrus, your paper, that which needs to be written. You will make the telephone calls and you will speak your truth one-to-one and in groups.

You know the evolution of collective consciousness into 5th dimension *is* going to be. It is going to happen. You can take heart from that. Some of you have been hoping, desiring, praying, and then at the same time thinking, "But not in my lifetime," and yet you are very, very close. The veil is growing thinner all the time, and there are more and more of ones such as you, of like mind, who are complete with the most intricate sandcastle. Now you are asking, "What is sand?"

You come from a place where there is allowance for ones to do their completion. You understand that, but at the same time, that does not keep you mute. You give hope. You give vision. You put it out there in front of other ones who are right on the verge of knowing their completion and wondering, "Where do I go from here? Do I go back to what I have always known, or do I go forward?" They do not even put that question into words. It is not even verbalized.

Then you come along and you say, "I have this vision. I know it will be, where ones will live in harmony and will respect each other, because we are of the same Creator, of the same Life principle. We are alive." If you can find no other common denominator, you can find that you are alive, right? You come along, and as the beholder you bring into 3rd dimensional consciousness a new perspective. Now, just because you love the other ones, which you do, and you recognize their divinity and you respect what they are completing, it does not mean that you have to be mute; it does not mean that you have to go off and take yourself to a monastery somewhere, which you have done previously in other lifetimes, or to take yourself to a cave way up in the mountains somewhere and to then commune with the divine masters as you have done in other lifetimes. This lifetime you have agreed to be the Beholder Activist. It is one of the more challenging roles to play because separated ego is going to say to you, "You'd better not say that. You've tried that before, and what happened? You were burned at the stake. What happened before? The head was asked of you."

The separated ego is also going to say, "What right do you have to suggest such an idea, that there could be harmony? Ones have always lived in groupings that had to defend themselves. It's always been that way. There's always been a leader, someone who could guide us, tell us where to go. What happens if we live in harmony and equality? Who's going to tell me what to do? Where is my security?" So separated ego is going to give you a listing of all kinds of problems, challenges, threats, warnings. That is okay. You take those questionings and warnings to the place of 5th dimensional perspective and you breathe, and you say, "That which has been, has been, but that does not mean it goes into the next moment." You are free, right now, of all past baggage. You are free, right now, of old past belief systems and self-images and image of what others and what the world had to be. If you will claim that freedom right now, beloved one, and you do, you are free, completely free.

We have spoken that there is going to be much of shift and change, some of the wings of the sandcastle collapsing. Count it all as good. Know that the old sandcastles have to come down before the new ones can even be contemplated, before the new ones can even be thought.

Allow yourselves to expect change. Allow yourselves to welcome change. Allow yourselves to be in that place of readiness that goes immediately to 5th dimensional perspective any time anything new comes to you. Take the deep breath and go to the place of holy vision. Then as you are guided, come back to this place that yet believes in a certain paradigm of collective belief and become the activist with a new perspective. That is what is being asked of you. Now it is time.

You will find yourself busier than ever and yet at peace, a very peaceful place of 5th dimension, being the beholder and yet being the activist; not to sit as the hermit—you have done that—but to read, to write, to speak, to act. And it does not have to be in "holy" words. In fact, if you are to speak sometimes with scriptural passages, ones will be at a place of closing their doors, the doors of the ears and heart. If you speak to them in the language which they understand, and they look to you and they relate, there is much of commonality and oneness that comes forth, and that, beloved one, is healing and evolutionary.

I would do with you again a meditation. I would do with you now what is called a coming to a place of peace. So allow yourself to take the deep breath and bring to mind something that has happened, either in the past twenty-four hours, or longer if you want to go back further, where there has been something that you would like to understand better, perhaps something that your news media has brought to you, perhaps something that a friend has said to you, perhaps something that the body has said to you. Allow yourself to bring to mind something that has been a question mark, perhaps a piece of information you have read and you wondered, "Is this true? And if this is true, what happens now?" Bring that to mind.

Taking another deep breath, expand the mind into the place of beholder, that place which is peaceful and open, willing and ready to receive, willing and ready to see expanded understanding.

Look upon what you have been contemplating and see if there is energy to it. See if there are colors that dance around with it. See if there is a path that leads from it, and where does that path go?

Sit with that question and ask of it as you would a master, "What is your message?"

Breathing deeply and easily, allow that question as the master to speak to you, to have a dialogue and to ask, "What more is there to know? Is there something that I need do? Is there something that I need to understand?"

Listen. Feel.

What is the feeling?

What is the path that it shows you?

Watch. Receive.

When you feel complete—you may take your time with this—when you feel complete, allow yourself the deep breath to re-energize the body; very slowly, very gently; bringing the information, the feeling, the visioning, with you. If there is more that you would know about this, know that any time you can come to this place and ask more.

And now, taking that deep breath, allow yourself to gently come back to this perspective, this reality that you call real—small "r"—bringing with you that sense of peace, that bit of information, whatever was given to you. Know that in that short time there was much that you touched upon, and you are not the same as you were before you went into that space.

That space is available to you at any time. Many of you know it well, because many of you have been pushed to the place where you felt you were in the corner and there could be no further backing up; you were against the rock and the hard place, and you have had to stop, to breathe, to ask, to go within. Just when you thought that there was no more help which could come to you, because you had prayed and you had hoped, in that moment a sense of divine peace descended upon you and it changed everything.

Then, as it will direct you, you take action. If you do not need to take action, then you abide for a while.

Beloved one, remember that space which is very expansive. Remember to go there often, for there are changes at hand, very good ones that you do not hear about on your news media because it loves to play up the dramas that seem to be the most tantalizing. But there is much at hand that is happening. You will see shifts that will be happening very soon, as I measure time, and perhaps sooner; in other words, I have heard it said that my time is a bit slow. Maybe it will fit in with your time.(Smile) There are changes that are coming, and they will ask of you, because you will ask it of yourself, to be the Beholder Activist, to go to that place of holy vision, and then from that place of understanding to be the activist, to help along the evolution of collective consciousness with your new vision.

So be it.

The True Religion

Beloved one, you are now at a great place in the collective evolution where there is a cycle of what I have called harvesting, a cycle where ones come to a completion and know themselves to be One with the Creative Power and are humbled by that remembrance and that knowing. Then, *because* you have been humbled and you have been in awe of what the divine creative power is, you have chosen to come and tap on the shoulder the brothers and sisters who are yet playing in the sandbox of duality and to say to them, "Look, I have had revelation; I have had remembrance. There *is* something more than just this sandbox. There *is* something more than just throwing sand at each other. There *is* something more than just building the sand castles that the wind and the rain will blow away. I have had remembrance."

So you come one more time to ask the questions, first of yourself and then of others, so that there can be the realization of At-one-ment. You have come through a very rich lineage of experience and expression of the divine. You have been the ones, even in a short time of what we will call your last two thousand years, who have known great illumination. You have been the ones who have been pure of heart, who have known from my teachings and the teachings of other great masters the remembrance of Who you are and What you are. You were illumined by the remembrance.

You brought forth great creativity as the ones who were known as the Gnostics, the ones who knew. You questioned what some of the other groupings who wanted power were putting forth as truth, and they did not appreciate your questioning. Sometimes you were requested to release the body, and you did, but that did not stop you; you recycled, you came back again, because the illumined ones always will come and resurface.

You have been the ones known as the divine illuminati. You have been the ones who have been the Gnostics, the ones who have been illumined. You have been the ones who have known the divine usage of the illumined knowledge, and you have also known the thread of ones who would use that illumined divinity in a way which was touched by world power—tainted, perhaps.

The divine illuminati are very much present at this time, and again, as you still have belief in duality, there are two threads which have diverged from one point, the illumined

Intelligence—capital "I". The threads diverged, where ones knowing the power of creativity and how to manipulate it have used it for personal gain or for greater gain of their grouping, and alternately, ones such as you are, illumined, and yet seemingly quiet about it, seemingly not as powerful.

Yet, you are *more* powerful, because the truly illumined ones, as I have said, will resurface over and over to anchor the light, to *be* the light, to *be* the illumined ones who recognize the brothers and sisters of the divine illuminati and watch how they yet use the power in world affairs, for there is much that is going on behind the scenes which is used for personal wealth and power. You are the divine illuminati, pure and undefiled, who recognize the Christ even in the ones who are doing the machinations behind the scenes. All power is given unto the illumined ones. How it is used—it is as we have spoken many times: the play, the stage, the scripting, the improv.

Some of the ones who are illuminati and do not realize that they are, and feel themselves to be in positions of power behind the scenes, are going to experience a "road to Damascus" experience where there is going to be for them an experience of a blinding light, a revelation, and it is going to upheave everything around them.

There is much in your world that wants everything to stay as it is. There is power in the status quo and in having power handed down from one generation of special interest to another generation of special interest, but that is going to be changing. You have already seen some of the crumbling of ones of individual wealth and power, and of groupings known as your corporations and business, where that which they thought they were doing for personal gain, without thought how it would affect others, have experienced a light upon the

workings, and a lot of it has crumbled. You are bringing forth
light to shine upon that which has been hidden for many,
many, centuries.

You have come through what is even called in your history
books the Dark Ages, where there was not too much of light.
The illumined ones, yes, such as you, came and lived the daily
lives, and you saw the beauty of our holy Mother, the Earth,
and you raised the families as best you could, but the overall
consciousness was not much enlightened.

Now there is more light. There are many who have agreed
to come at this time to be the lightbearers, to be the ones who
are as bridges for remembrance, such as you; the ones who
have been seeking, wanting to know, asking "Where do we go
from here, where have I been, where am I now?"—wanting to
know the Christ purpose of everything. You have now what
you would call assistance from other dimensions—masters,
guides, teachers, and angels, much of what you yet see to be
outside help, and yet it is not outside of you; it is very much
you, as you understand an expanded aspect of you. You are the
ones who ask the tough questions; you are the ones who will
speak out from the grass roots and say, "I want to know the
true religion. I want to know not just the religion of the
churches; I want to know not just the religion of my family,
the old belief systems, but I want to know the *true* religion.

The root word of religion is *religio*, meaning to be bound
together as one, and that has been forgotten. As you have seen
in the short time of the last two thousand years, there has been
much division, splintering.

There were on the one hand, you, the Gnostics, who remembered the divinity, the light within. You knew your connection with the Father. On the other hand, there were the ones

who took the teachings and revelations and put them into a package that then was given to brothers and sisters, and it was given in a way that, "This is what is true, correct; you must believe it." You, as the Gnostics, said, "But it is too limited. The package does not include all."

The ones who liked the package allowed the manipulation to spread through fear, guilt, and ignorance, until one came along whom you know well: Martin Luther. He knocked upon the door and he said, "Open the door. There is more." Then from that opening of a door, there was a splintering of more and more doors opening, and as the doors opened, more boxes were made.

Because of generational teaching, you were indoctrinated through family belief that you would be a Catholic; you would be a Lutheran; you would be the Anglican; you would be the Baptist; you would be the Presbyterian; you would be the Christian Scientist; you would be so many, divided from the One, to the place where now many of you have thrown out everything and said, "No, there has to be an inclusive religion, which is not exclusive; it has to be inclusive."

When I was with you as the one known as Yeshua, it was asked of me, "What is the greatest commandment?" I said unto you, and you have it recorded in your holy Scriptures, that the greatest commandment is to love the Lord thy God with all your heart, all your soul, and all your mind. Now, what does that mean? To love the Lord your God means to remember your divinity.

You are desiring now to know that place of great love and to bring yourself into the remembrance of the Lord God of your being, the divinity of you, and to love that with all your heart and with all your soul.

All that you have ever experienced is held within what you call the individuated soul. All of the experiences of all the lifetimes go into that conceptual package, and yet it does not have boundaries. But within this point of focus, this time, you have claimed for yourself an individuated soul with all of the experiences of all of the lifetimes that you have ever had in that totality, to love the divinity of yourself with all your heart, all your soul, and all your mind.

What does it mean to love the Lord your God with your mind? It means, in other words, to *use* your mind; not just to be led as sheep, but to use the mind to know the creativity, the divinity of you, to question Where you have come from and Who you are, and to know oneness with the Lord God of your being.

Then I said unto you, "And the second commandment is as the first: to love your neighbor as yourself." For when you know your true Self—capital "S"—when you come into the place of the remembrance of the divinity of you, you see the divinity of the other one as well. You love your neighbor as yourself, because you know your neighbor *is* yourself, an aspect of the one Self—choices and decisions and behaviors, you love that one, the Christ of that one, because it is You.

That is the true religion. You come to the place of realizing, truly realizing—making real in your awareness—great love of the Lord God of your being; great love of the divinity of Self and of the neighbor, wherever the neighbor may be; perhaps sitting next to you, or perhaps halfway around the planet, our holy Mother, the Earth. The true religion follows one rule, and you know this rule very well. It is golden: to do unto others as you would have them do unto you.

When mankind/womankind come to the place where there is realization that, "I truly walk in the sandals of everyone else I see and can think of, and even ones beyond my ken," then you will understand the divinity of One and will understand and put into practice, manifest, the Golden Rule. That is the true religion.

Apply the Golden Rule. Live in the true religion; not the religion which has been handed down to you in the boxes. Already those religions are outdated. But live from the knowing that, "I am walking in the sandals of my brother, my sister. How would I want to be treated, regarded, respected?" And from that place, stir yourself and get very busy to help them. Stir yourself to say in the right ears what needs to be said to change things.

As you live from that space, know you that all power, even as it has been twisted and manipulated in the past, will be transformed. All power will be given unto you in heaven and on Earth. It has to be, because the power comes from heaven. It comes from the divinity of you, and you are the bridges who are living this reality; therefore, you can and will transform the world. You *are* powerful.

Allow yourself to welcome change, because there are going to be changes. Allow yourself to get caught up in the so-called drama of it, and then to step back from it, the same as you do as you watch the drama on your television set or your videos, your movies. You can get quite caught up in what is going on; you can get right on the edge of your chair, right to the edge of your heart.

And then you take a deep breath and you say, "Ah, but it is a story." Yes, it is a story; yes, you are involved in it; and yes, you can step back from it for a moment to behold with holy vision and to appreciate the drama of it; to come to a place where you can speak your remembrance of holy vision into the ears which need to be spoken into.

You stand at a pivotal, most wonderful place. You have heard me say this other times, for it is not that there is just one point in time that is pivotal. It is, as you understand time, a process. So yes, I have said this before. It is a most wonderful time now, a pivotal time in your history, in the evolution of collective consciousness, where you have the power, you have the remembrance, you have the desire to make changes and to live the true religion, coming from the place of the Golden Rule, accepting the brothers and sisters as aspects of the one Self.

It does not mean that you agree with their decisions or their choices of behavior, but you accept them as aspects of the one Self and you love them as the Self. And you get very busy, as the guidance directs you, to bring about more of the remembrance of love. Live from the place of love, for that *is* the true religion; not conditional love which dictates, "You have to be of my religion, of my family, of my language, of my country, of my workplace, of my skin color;" but the place of true, expansive, unconditional Love which turns the page to a new script.

Do unto others as you would have them do unto you.

So be it.

Sacred Union

I would speak with you now of a topic which is near and dear to my heart. I would speak with you about love. I would speak with you, first, about human love, which is most wonderful. You find that love in the friendships; you find that love in the relationships which you make on a committed level. I would also speak with you about divine love; about sacred union.

You have much which has been coming up in many of your books, even in some of your videos and movies; much which is coming up that would suggest that I had relationship with woman, and I did. I knew woman. I knew Mary Magdalene very well. She was my wife.

It was commonly accepted in that time that as rabbi I would be married. If in those times I would be rabbi and not married, it would have been something unusual. Truly, I was married, and truly there were children.

You have books now which have been teasing the mind, asking questions as to, "What do you believe about one Jesus', one Jeshua's life?" You have been finding resonance within yourself with certain truths as they have been spoken to you or written about, and you have been finding a resonance of saying, "Yes, that does make sense to me. I believe that. Of course. How would he come and relate to us as human if he did not know all of human life?"

Good question to ask. For indeed, I did come, as you have come, many times to know human life, to know human relationships, to know human challenges, and to remember, as you have been doing, what it means to be humanly divine and divinely human.

So there has been much which has been coming to light about relationships and about my relationship. I will say unto you that it takes nothing away from my message. In truth, it adds everything to my message. However, it has been written in what you have compiled as the holy Scriptures, and has been commonly accepted, that I was the very Son of God and that to know woman and to have family would be sinful. But you have wondered in some lifetimes when you have been taught that because you were married and you knew the mate, and you had children, that you were sinful. And yet when you looked upon the newborn, you asked, "What is sinful about this? What can be sinful about the newborn and the process of bringing forth the newborn?"

So you have a time now when you are contemplating much of what it means to be in love and what love is all about. Love truly is your nature. It is expansive. We have spoken of this many times, that as you know human love you know an expansion that goes beyond self. You lose yourself in the love with another one. For a moment or so or longer you are able to step into another one's sandals and to be inside of them. You lose all sense of small self in the love which you have with them.

Divine love is even more than that. Human love is as a pointer, a signpost perhaps, which points in the direction of what divine love is, and you are divine Love expressing even within the focus of the specificity of individuality, that which you have chosen as your individual expression. You are divine Love, you are expansive, and you are expanding all the time. The one Mind is forever creating, forever expanding, forever expressing, and will continue to expand, even beyond the concept of time, to know Itself. You are forever creating.

There is much that is coming to the forefront of your questioning as to relationship and what it means to be in relationship with others, and I would say to you that truly you have many in your society in this day and time, as was true in the time when I walked the holy Mother Earth, who are pushing the envelope, as it is called, pushing the boundaries.

You have much which is now of controversial nature, and yet it is of divine nature, where ones who are activating the same gender body are finding love with one another and wanting to have that expression sanctified by society; ones who are saying, "Look, we have deep love, the same as the man/woman, woman/man relationship. We have deep love for each other, and we want that acknowledged." I will say unto you that those voices will not be stilled until there is realization of the love which has bound them together, the same as with man and woman.

Ones are expressing love to each other in ways that the church, the holy fathers, did not sanctify, and yet love goes beyond what the arbitrary rules of society or culture would dictate. You have many of the ones in this day and time who are standing up for the love which they feel for another beyond appearances, coming from the place of the heart to be as teachers, not allowing the voice to be silent any longer, but coming forth and saying, "Love is love, and I love my partner."

As you have acknowledged that you have lived many lifetimes, you have activated many forms of life, and you have activated the male gender form, you have activated the female gender form, and in some lifetimes you have been attracted very much to one of same gender, and you found ways to be with that one as would be accepted by culture. Now ones are coming to a place where they are pushing out the boundaries of what present culture has said should be or has to be.

The holy fathers of the church selected the writings which you have in your holy Scriptures, and they selected the writings according to what they felt would be the best for the continuance of their belief. Since there is usually no issue of progeny from ones of same gender, it was seen to be favorable that you have male/female marriage union so that there could be the offspring, more and more of the offspring who would then be servants of the church, either direct servants or the ones who would give of their tithes, etc. So it was seen to be beneficial for the continuance of the establishment that what would be favored would be the marriage between man and woman. But as you have, in your own thinking, come to discern, love cannot be limited to just one form.

Many now are having the courage to stand up and to voice the love which is in their hearts and to bring that forth so that other ones can see that they are family as well. Many of the ones who are visible in your certain gatherings do have families. They are of same gender and they are making a family unit. They are pushing out the boundaries of what has been for a long time accepted as being the only way that God would look with favor upon marriage.

But sacred union, marriage, happens whenever there is love. It matters not the form of the body. What matters is in the heart, for out of the heart come the issues of life, the emotions, the love, the caring, the sharing.

So I say unto you that sacred union is to be found from heart to heart, not body to body. Bodies are temporary. Love is always. The love which one feels for another does not cease when the body is released. That love is stored in what you know as the Akashic records. That love is always there, part of the divine Mind, part of the divine Being that you are, and will always be there.

Bodies come and go, but not the love relationships. The more that you open up the heart to love, the more that love will be understood, felt, recognized, expressed and experienced. But I say unto you that which you have already been coming to discern yourselves —for you are ones who are of allowing minds —you are ones who have been challenged sometimes by the family members or friends who would be speaking out from a place that is a bit different than what society would say, and you have found yourself having to examine issues which you have taken for granted many lifetimes.

Now you have come to a place of allowance, and you have said, "Well, what is right for one, if they find love in that relationship, so be it." So I speak to you of something which you have truly already discerned, but I would take it a step further. I would say that sacred union, marriage if you will, does not have to be with the paperwork. It does not have to be condoned, sanctified by society or by culture. It is, in truth, the place where you come to acknowledge the sacredness of self and relationship with self, where you know the masculine/feminine attributes of self, and you bring into conscious awareness a wholeness, holiness, and you know sacred union, marriage, within the self.

You come to that place where you acknowledge that, "I am All. I have been male/female. I have been every living form upon this planet. All of the attributes which I recognize in others are within me as well; otherwise, I would not see them."

Truly, what you are coming to know is the sacred union of wholeness, the place where you acknowledge that you are androgynous. You are both male and female. You have the attributes of the whole, and you recognize within yourself that these are coming to a place of balance in the expression of the being of you. It is called recognizing the Christ, that place of holiness, that place of divine wholeness, and allowing yourself to celebrate the sacred union of all creative abilities of self.

You stand now at a place where it is beneficial that you acknowledge the wholesomeness and holiness of divine Self, which you are, so that you can then project that knowing to your world, for your world is very much in separation, in boxes, in categories, in labels. If you look just at appearance, there is much that separates one culture from another, brother from brother, sister from sister.

As you are coming to the place of acknowledging the sacred union of all aspects within yourself, you can look with the eyes of the Christ upon the world, and you can speak words of healing which the world so much needs to know in this day and time.

You have cultures that are warring against each other, cultures that are each right as they understand rightness to be. You stand at the brink of a holy war once again where, because of generational thinking, ones are going to stand up for what they have been taught has to be the right way and the right expression of cultural, societal laws. You are standing right now at the brink of the potential of another holy war, as it has been called, although there is nothing truly holy about war, because it is divisive.

So it behooves you to claim sacred union within yourself, sacred marriage of all aspects of the self, and to be able to speak from the Christ self of you to the others who would yet see separation, to speak from a place which fosters dialogue. For truly, each culture believes in the rightness of the generational teaching. They "know" that they are "right." It has been taught to them down through generations; therefore, it must be true — as *you* have stood many lifetimes in your truth and you have done battle with other ones who would assail, as you saw the threat, your truth, and you have done battle with them to the place of requesting that they lay down the body, or they requested of you that you lay down the body. What was gained from that? Well, you got to turn the pages of scripting and do it again.

You have come to the place now where you have said, "Enough already. There has to be space, holy space, for dialogue. There has to be holy space where ones can meet to speak their truth in the space where they begin to have understanding of other's position." That is the first step: recognizing the Christ of the other one, allowing space for dialogue, and speaking to the necessity for dialogue. For as I have said, you stand on the brink of ones wanting to hold to their truth so strongly that they will release the body, to have to recycle — perhaps recycle back into the same culture to do it over and over again — until there are ones such as you who rise up from what would be known as the grass roots and say, "I acknowledge that you understand that you are right in your position. Let us speak about it. Let us make space."

You had recently one of your leaders [President Clinton] who was very good at bringing ones to the table to speak with each other. There did not come from those talks a resolution and a peace, but the leader was sincere of heart and had a charisma about him which would bring together ones of differing opinions so that they could meet and talk. This was a start, and it needs to be continued; not to have ones standing in separate camps with the embattlements and the banners and flags and whatever, as you have done down through the ages, saying, "I see you over there, and you are wrong. You must accept my truth, my package of truth as it is," but to have the openness of dialogue once again.

When you are in your time of meditation, when you are in your time of doing the daily activities of washing the dishes, taking the shower, driving the vehicle, allow your mind to seek out the minds of ones who are in position to make space for dialogue and suggest to them, for you are powerful in your suggestions. There is, in truth, no separation; that which you will put out on the ethers goes out to other ones and it is felt, it is received. So as you will be standing in a place of allowance, in a space which allows for dialogue, and as you suggest that to the ones who are in a place of making this happen, it will be a great wave of power, not as the world understands power, but a great wave of power which will impact what you see future events to be.

Now, as we have spoken many times, that which you put out is your gift freely given. Whether it is received or not is not your responsibility. You do not have power over whether it is received or not, but you do have power to give it as a gift. So I suggest that you come from the place of acknowledging wholeness within self, acknowledging that you have walked in the sandals of the brothers and sisters who now seem to be in far lands with different cultures, and that you now want to come to a place of dialogue, a place where there can be speaking — not judgment, but speaking — so that there can be understanding.

This applies not only to world situations that you see on a global scale, but it also applies to the workplace and to the family; again, allowing space for ones to speak their truth, not in judgment, but to be able to speak where they are coming from, and a safe space where they will not feel that as soon as they put a sentence out they will be jumped upon; but to have the acknowledgment that, "You are right in your position. It may not be as I see it, but you, I understand, are right as you see it to be. Let us speak with non-judgment. Let us dialogue."

There is much power in dialogue. There is much power in dialogue within the self as well, for as you are coming to the place of accepting the sacred union of the marriage within yourself, you will be doing much dialogue with the various aspects, as they seem to be distinct, within self, and coming to a place of peace and acceptance with some of the things that you have been taught were not acceptable, perhaps.

For you have all gone through a process of the molding and shaping with the parents, with the peers, with the society in which you have grown up. You have certain things that have been taught to you that are the good attributes and some that are not so good, and yet this is all part of humanhood, and it is time to embrace, to accept in the sacred place, all of the aspects of human experience — all of the aspects — not to judge, but to have dialogue with those aspects and to love those aspects to the place where you can have free dialogue without judgment; not to judge when you have a certain feeling of confusion or of anger, to say, "I don't want to feel that," but to say, "Where does that feeling come from? How can I see this anew? How can I see this with holy vision? How can I come to a place of knowing sacred union within myself so that I can then project that as example to the world?" Then you come to a place where you allow space for a moment or so — or longer — where whatever you are feeling, you have dialogue with it–"Why do I feel...what does this truly come from, this feeling? What is it based in? How does it serve me? What do I want to see be the fruit of these feelings?" And in nonjudgment you have the space of acknowledging, as you do when you come into a marriage with a partner, to have space to look at the various treasures of the attributes; not to judge them, but to say, "Oh, I never really looked at things that way." When you are with another, and they say something that is totally off the wall — or at least you think it may be — you can say, "Well, I never thought about it that way. Let me think about that."

Then there is opportunity for dialogue which allows you to understand a different point of view. You have choice to incorporate it into your understanding, which oftentimes does happen, because you have then expanded to the place where you do understand where they are coming from, or not. But at least you have made space to acknowledge the various perspectives.

Each one of you comes to any subject from a different point of view, a different perspective because of past lifetimes, because of present lifetime experiences, and because of cell memory held within the body, with which you are doing improv from time to time to change that memory.

Now, oftentimes when ones come to the table, they come with the blinders on and they can only see a limited view. They are a bit in the box, so to speak. But as there will be space for continuing dialogue, the blinders expand in opening, and you begin to be able to walk in the sandals of another one and to understand what has brought them to a place that previously you would have judged to be wrong, and you begin to see the treasure of Allness. That is what these times are all about.

You stand on the brink of much change, and separated ego does not like change. But the I Am Ego celebrates change as expansion, as treasure. Already you are seeing much which is coming to light; much that was swept under the carpet, seemingly, which has come out for the light to shine upon it, not always in such a favorable light.

Yet the ones whom you would judge harshly are your servants, for they have brought those issues to your awareness. They have played their parts well. And yes, you can say that what they have chosen would not be in the most harmony and upliftment, but yet they have served the upliftment of the collective consciousness in bringing those issues right out into the open.

Every day there are new issues which come to light that others would like to keep quiet, and yet the very stones cry out the truth, and the evidence comes to light. Then what you do with that is most wonderful improv. You go through a habitual process of judgment; it is a reaction, but it is habitual, and since it is habit, it can be changed to where you have begun to wonder, "How could others do what they did? What were they thinking? Why would they feel that they could do, should do, must do, or have the freedom to do what was done?"

You begin in that questioning to expand your own understanding of what we have talked about as the sacred union of self in understanding all aspects of the human self; not only yourself as you see it individualized, but the human self, collective; and you begin to have a little more space to understand what is behind what is being shown to you, and at some point in time you will say with great joy, "Aha, it is myself who has done this, and I celebrate even that which I would have judged. I celebrate it as the expression of creativity — not creativity, perhaps, that is in the short term uplifting, but creativity that is in the long term leading to the Atonement."

Now, I speak to you here of absolute Truth, which is hard to fit into the box of world understanding, of human understanding, but I speak from a place of absolute Truth because you have asked to know. It does not mean that you are going to instantly be in that place of understanding and celebrating absolute Truth, but it does mean that it is as catalyst that will put you forward some pages in the scripting; in other words, you can flip over some of the pages to where you come to an acknowledgment of the divine Self and you know, "It is myself who has done this." It is from a place of non-judgment, because you begin to understand all. Then you love self, and you claim in that moment the sacred union with all aspects of Self, not in judgment, but in a place of understanding the divine creativity, the freedom of creativity, and all of the infinite variety of creativity that you bring forth even into this finite focus of Christed energy.

You stand at a place now where sacred union of all aspects of self is most beneficial to the weathering of the next few years, to the blossoming and the fruit of the next few years. This is why I spoke to you starting with the specific example of my life and the sacred union that I knew with Mary Magdalene, how I knew human life, and I do know it; it was my contract, the same as yours. I spoke to you of how sacred union is not just between male and female as the bodies, but it comes from the love that is felt, that is honored and acknowledged, and how this love does not end with the body. When the body is released, the love remains.

I spoke to you of finding that sacred union within yourself, incorporating, celebrating all aspects of yourself, the male attributes and the feminine, and coming to a balance. You have much that has been spoken in previous years of the divine feminine and the celebration of the goddess. It is time now to bring all of those attributes into balance, into incorporation within the claiming and understanding of your own expression, to acknowledge as you are activating the male body, "I am the goddess in expression, as well," and to claim as you are activating the feminine body, "I am the male aspects of the god self, as well," and to bring all into harmony, into balance, into expression, into acknowledgment, into the sacred union of the whole. And then there is gifting of holy vision from which you offer to the world your understanding of the acknowledgment of sacred union of *all* beings so that there can be dialogue. For truly, everyone who activates the body is the divine spark of light; otherwise, they would not be activating the body. Even the brothers who are most limited in their understanding of what is right or wrong are seeking at a very deep level to know their own wholeness and their relationship to wholeness.

As you will be abiding in that place of sacred union within yourself and speaking in your quiet times in the meditation to the ones who are in position to make space for dialogue, you are bringing forth healing to the world, a healing that truly is going to bring about that which has been prophesied as to the knowing of heaven upon earth, knowing equality, honor, and respect for all beings.

As you have looked upon your world in these days, that is not what you see. But what you hold as a seed within your heart will come to be, because you will be nurturing it from the place of the Christ within. Hold that seed. Hold that vision. Know that truly there will be changes. There will be times that appearances will seem to be contrary to what you would say would be holy, harmonious, enlightened, and yet know you that everything serves the Atonement. We have spoken that to you many times.

Acknowledge within yourself love of self, of all parts of your being. Acknowledge love as you see the brothers and sisters. Acknowledge the mirror and the love that you can find in the mirror that they show you. Acknowledge that there *is* love in the world, for there *is* love that is crying out to be expressed, to be honored once again. And know that, truly, that which you have as a seed in the heart will be nurtured by your understanding and acknowledgment of sacred marriage within Self, the one Self that we are.

So be it.

I Will Not Leave You Comfortless

In a time which you see to be long ago, I spoke to you that I would have to go away from you for awhile, and I told you that I would not leave you comfortless. This is true. I spoke to you that I would not leave you comfortless, and I will not. I will come unto you any time you call me. You have called, and I have been there; perhaps not in the way which you expected or hoped for, or in the way ones had said to you that one Jesus has to come, but I have been there with you. Perhaps I have spoken through a friend. Perhaps I have spoken in your mind and given you an idea which perhaps you did not label as coming from Jesus because your idea of Jesus and what He would do was a bit different.

Any time you have questions, call upon me and I will come to you. Any time you are wrestling with a knotty question that seems to be full of the tangles and you cannot see your way clear with it, call to me and I will come to you.

Whenever you are wanting comfort, call upon me and I will come. It is a promise which I made to you in what you would see as years past. It is a promise which I renew to you in this day and time.

It is a promise which *you* may give to others as you see them struggling; not that they need to call upon one Jesus, but that they may call upon you. You find yourself being the comforter, for such as is given to you, you give unto others.

When you struggle and you wonder, "What is it all about?" ask for the Comforter, and then remember the power in the breath and *breathe*. When you ask for the Comforter, remember to breathe, and as you take that deep breath, what do you feel? Calm. You feel the peace which comes with that deep breath. Then allow yourself to step into the place of the beholder; not the place of the doer; not the place of the person who has all of the answers or must be expected to have all of the answers, but the person, the entity, the energy of the one beholder who watches. That which you have been troubled about, you will see with new perspective.

The beholder is at peace, and in that peace there is great comfort.

We have spoken in other times how it is very easy to get caught up in the activities of daily living: the relationships, the employment, the various innuendoes of the world. It is very easy to get caught up to the place where your comfort disappears momentarily.

We have spoken of the simplicity and the power of the deep breath. It is the first thing which you do when you take the individual life upon this plane. It is the first thing that the newborn physical child does: breathe. It is the last thing that you do as you decease the body.

The power of the breath goes with this life experience hand in hand. Therefore, as you are working with anything within this physical realm, anything within the human experience, remember to consciously breathe. It does not have to be done with a certain ritual. You do not have to sit with the legs crossed in a certain position. You do not have to hold one nostril, breathe through one and then exhale through the other. You do not have to be facing the west or east or north or south. You do not have to be breathing incense.

All you have to do is breathe consciously, wherever you find yourself to be. In that moment of drawing in the breath, you allow the Comforter to be known, to nurture you, to hold you, to give you revelation and wisdom. In that moment of the deep breath when you bring in the Comforter, I will come and abide with you in that space of peace. I will not leave you comfortless, ever. I will come to you whenever you call.

Within this most wonderful flow of divine Energy which you are, within this most wonderful realm of physicality and physical creations, within this most wonderful lifetime which you are fashioning for yourself, remember to pause often and to ask for comfort; to ask for holy wisdom; to ask for me to be with you. It is my great pleasure to come to you.

Know you that you have brought forth most wonderful works of creation? Know you that it is celebratory to have done that? It is worth celebrating. Know you that you are a part, even as you see yourself to be individual, of a vast extension of creativity which is expanding past all limits, past all time, past all concepts, past all imagination? That is how wonderful you are. Catch hold of that Truth. Be happy to be a part of it. Be happy to be the point of light in the great Mosaic, and yet know yourself to be the Mosaic itself, for there is no separation. The one Mind sees and knows the Mosaic, and the one Mind yet asks, "What more?" in Its expansion. Catch hold of the excitement of that.

You see the drama in your life and in others' lives around you, but there is much more than that. Every day, every moment is a point of light within the Mosaic. Every lifetime is a point of light within the Mosaic. The Mosaic itself is this reality and more, and you are at once the individual and the All.

Remember to abide in the place of the beholder, for the beholder gives you the picture of more of the Mosaic. You will see this lifetime and the ones who activate bodies in this day and time. You will see ones both incarnate and discarnate, and you will see how they are joined, as you are, in the stream of Life and Life expression, light and beyond light, in dimensions which are expanding and expressing beyond anything you can imagine in this point of focus. They are part of the Mosaic, as you are, too.

Do you begin to get an idea of how vast you are? Do you begin to get a clue? Do you? Let no one say to you that you live an ordinary life. Let no one, including yourself, say to you that you are just a small bit, living out certain years, and that there is no meaning.

Breathe. Behold. Imagine the Mosaic, and then allow the edges of the Mosaic to be dissolved and see it in Its vastness. See your part in it and see yourSelf in the stream of the consciousness of divine Being, ever going forward, ever expanding; expressing; experiencing; knowing; and asking, "What more?"

I will not leave you comfortless. In Truth, I cannot, for the Comforter is always with you; it is the Holy Spirit, your Spirit of holiness, your divinity.

I will not leave you comfortless. I will give you a new vision of yourSelf: the Mosaic of One which we create together.

I will not leave you comfortless. Call upon me, and I will come. You are my beloved.

So be it.

My Peace I Give Unto You

Beloved one, the world will speak to you of trials and tribulations, challenges and decisions, worries, things which must be attended to, but I speak to you of your divine nature. I speak to you of joy, the joy of the Father which is you come forth into form, into this reality, to bring His light and love into this reality that yet believes that there could be otherwise. Shall we have some fun together?

I have heard you speaking of the heaviness of the world, of the decisions and choices which seemingly may have been made without your agreement. I have seen you struggling, crying to the heavens for understanding and for holy vision. Now, we have spoken previously about your Reality—capital "R"—the Reality where you abide interdimensionally, the Reality which does not focus specifically upon any dimension or any expression, but knows Itself to be the Isness of All: the interdimensionality, the true Being of you. From that place of interdimensionality you draw forth, because of your creative nature and your creative power, all realities to play with them.

Indeed, if you adopt for yourself the attitude that the reality where you find yourself to be is but a play, it will allow you the deep breath both on the physical level and the spiritual level to then move into holy vision.

In truth, what you are playing with is a most wonderful scenario. You have agreed that as individuated consciousness you will be part of a collective consciousness which is desiring to know change, which is desiring to know Reality—capital "R"—brought even into a reality—small "r"—and to do a quantum shift over what you have seen to be eons of time of believing in small "r" reality. It takes a bit of expansion, it takes a bit of allowance, and it takes a whole lot of trust. You have had that tested and you will continue to call upon trust to affirm that, "That which I see happening in the world serves the Atonement," because it does.

Even though you would say that some decisions which are made, paths which are chosen, may not be the ones which you would choose, yet everything serves the Atonement. The collective consciousness of which you have agreed to be a part has chosen a certain pathway, a journey if you will, a journey without distance, and yet it seems to be a very long journey back to the remembrance of Reality—capital "R".

Chapter 19

So count all things as good even though they may not look in one moment to be what you would judge to be good. Count all to be good. Believe in the best. Trust in the holy vision.

You will be seeing much of change. It is time. You have decreed that you want change. Therefore, when the holy Child decrees, it will be unto you as you have decreed, but not in a way that the small ego fears. When you speak of change, small ego resists, runs and hides and says, "Please, don't change. I don't like the way things are right now but I'm sure I'm not going to like change. So let's stay with what's familiar."

You are going to see choices which seem to go counter to what you would choose. You are going to see—you have already seen and heard—the rattling of the sabers. In the world historically you have had wars and rumors of war, and yet the higher Intelligence of the collective, the higher Intelligence of you, from which you are not separate, will not allow destruction of this planet. Yes, there will be changes in the world, but not the Earth.

You have wondered about that because you have known that there is power in your technology which has brought into the hands of some the seeming ability to bring about destruction. There will be the possibility considered, but it will not destroy the planet. There is a higher Intelligence which is working throughout the choices that are made.

When the world is too much with you, abide with me. Allow yourself the deep breath. Seek me in that breath and know that always I abide with you. Know that always I am here for you. No matter what you are looking at, no matter what you are facing, know that you can come unto me and find the peace that *I* abide within, and know that that peace is yours as well.

Take the deep breath. Take a deep breath right now. Feel how that allows the body even to expand. You individually have been taking shallow breaths, focusing upon what you need to attend to, what might happen, what you had to be prepared for. You have been breathing for the most part at a very shallow level. Allow yourself as often as you can remember to take the deep breath, and in that breath come and abide with me. Find the peace that I give unto you.

I say this to you because it is an important balancing point for you. It will be a place you will come unto many times because the world is going to be very much with you and you with it, for there are going to be changes. There are going to be what seem to be manipulations. There are going to be what you see as maneuvers, compromises that do not look upon the surface to be all that they should be. The world is going to be very much in your focus, and you are going to be in the focus of the world, as well, because you have agreed that you will be a balancing energy.

You are the sensitives, you are the ones who feel energy changes. You are the ones who feel the changes before they are manifest. You are the ones who have often volunteered to be present at the ushering in of a new age, a time of the leap in the evolution of the collective consciousness. What you are looking at now is another one of those leaps in consciousness, and you have agreed that you will be here for it and that you will help the evolution because you are sincere of purpose and pure of heart; and not so lacking in intelligence either. (Smile)

Allow yourself, when the world is too much with you, to take the deep breath no matter where you are and to receive the peace that I give unto you. For whenever you find me, you find peace. Whenever you find me, you find joy. Whenever you find me, you find divine purpose and holy vision. Even as you then turn and look at the world, you see things through new eyes.

Allow yourself to receive the peace that I give unto you. Seek me. My peace I give unto you; not as the world gives, because the world gives and then takes away, changes, or says there has to be condition. My peace I give unto you unconditionally. It is always there for you.

Anytime you will ask for it, you know the way in. It is through the breath. My peace I give unto you.

Now, in that place of peace there will be intuition. There will be a knowing of other realities, other possibilities. There will be a feeling that comes to you from time to time of living in more than one reality. It can be disconcerting to an ego which has said, "This is what I want, a box. I want to know the parameters of the box. I am going to stay within the box and that is all I am going to now allow."

But you have already opened out the sides of the box. You have already allowed the blinders that the ego would put on to be opened out so that you see much more. You walk into other realities from time to time, and the ego will bring you back and it will say, "Where have you been? Come back here and worry." You know that voice very well.

But you can say unto the ego, because the ego—the small ego—is of your making, "One moment, please. I desire to abide in peace. I desire to know expanded vision. I desire to breathe just for one moment." And who can measure a moment? It can be a lifetime, can it not? My peace I give unto you, and the ego cannot take it from you.

You are standing collectively and also individually at a most wonderful threshold, and it is scary to the separated ego.

You are standing on the threshold of moving into a place of claiming expanded reality. Now, when I say that, I yet use the lower case "r", but it is a reality which allows that there can be many realities abiding side by side and time by time within time, for there are within this moment many realities. I speak to you. You hear the words. You hear my voice. You hear the message. You feel my love. You feel my peace. But I also speak at the same moment in other realities to ones that you would see to be other than you, and yet they are you, aspects of the One. They are here right now with you, right in this same space where you see yourself to be, and yet they are but a veil away. It is very thin, the belief which separates you from knowing other realities that are right within your midst.

You are coming to a place where there is going to be the acceptance of expanded reality. You will know visitation from some of the intelligence from space—some of the brothers, some of the most wonderful spaceships. I will come and visit you in what you see to be yet manifest—thought manifest—as a spaceship.

You will see ones running in terror because of habitual belief. You will see others stand in wonderment because of remembrance of space intelligence, space unitedness. If you take a deep breath, you will abide with me in that space of One.

Do you see what I meant when I suggested we have some fun together? What we are doing, and have been doing for some time, is to take the specific focus of what you have believed collectively and individually to be the allness of you, the truth—small "t"—of you. We have been suggesting that perhaps the allness of you is a bit larger than what you have thought it to be, and that you can be comfortable in that expansion, not having to fear it, but feeling comfortable in the expansion; in truth, coming to a place which you have longed for, a place where you feel accepted, loved, nurtured, held in the expansion of that love. Once you have felt that Love, once you have felt that peace, there is remembrance, and no matter how separated ego, no matter how the world will clamor, there is no going back from that place of peace.

Yes, the ego will come and tug at the mind. The ego will say, "But, master, shouldn't you be doing something about this?" And you say, "One moment, please." One deep breath.

I share with you my excitement for you, because truly what you are moving into is what you have prayed for, wished for, hoped for, and brought forth even in manifest form, even in other realities in what you would see to be other lifetimes.

There is an excitement which is as the simmering at the bottom of the pot, and you have felt it: an excitement, an anticipation, a waiting, a hoping for something that you did not quite know what it was going to be; and still you do not quite know what it is going to be, and I cannot tell you that yet either because you are great masters of the improv. But I can tell you that it is going to be for the Atonement and that it is going to be for the expansion of the collective consciousness into a new reality which allows the heavy blanket that has been upon the collective consciousness for so long to be lightened by the enlightenment of your remembrance of how it feels to abide in peace.

Whenever you feel the heavy blanket of the world, allow yourself to return quickly unto me. Return quickly to the place of peace within. Trust it. Claim it. Know it. Know that it is your divine nature to be peace, to be joyful in that peace, and to trust that all things work for the Atonement.

I will not say that all things work to the good because that brings in judgment of what is good and what is not so good, but all things work for the Atonement, the place of realization of the At-one-ment where the holy Child realizes, "I am not separate from the Father. I am the extension of the Father come into this point of reality to play, to be within a scripting that, yes, has much of improv in it, much of twists and turns, and yet it is a play." As one of your beloved masters has written, "The play's the thing," is it not?

Remember that as you hear your news media giving you all of the breaking news. What does it break? It breaks your peace. If you attend to it, it is breaking news. It is well named, because if you attend to it in the way that they hope that you will so that they can sell more of their products, it breaks your knowing of peace. So when the world is too much with you, breathe and come unto me and abide with me for a moment, and allow that moment to spill out over into the next moment and the next moment.

You are going to see changes in leadership. The collective consciousness is doing a shuffling of the cards, and you are going to see changes. You are going to see that which has been seemingly hidden—some policies, practices, maneuverings that have been seemingly done in secret—come out into the open more and more. Everything is going to be brought to the light. Every practice that has not come from a place of holiness, a place of love, a place of compassion, a place of oneness with my brother, my sister; every practice and every grouping that has agreed to the practice is going to be brought into the Light.

Walk you carefully according to your own principle of truth and of love and of compassion. In other words, be in integrity as to what you choose to do, and do not judge others, although it will be very easy, but allow the holy vision.

When ones come to you troubled, frightened, weary, ask them, "Would you be willing to breathe with me?" They will, and in that moment, in the simplicity of the deep breath, in the sacred moment of the breath, my peace I will give unto you and to them as a healing. For your world calls out for healing. Your bodies call out for healing. Your emotional bodies call out for healing even as the collective soul calls out for healing now at this time. My peace I give unto you with the simplicity of the willingness to take the deep breath.

Breathe with me. Abide with me. You have that saying in your holy Scriptures and in some of your songs—"Abide with me." Allow yourself to translate that into "Breathe with me." As you will breathe with me, you will abide with me. With the breath, you bring in the inspiration of spirit, and it will make all things new. Abide with me. Breathe with me.

Allow yourself to know that everything which is upturned is as the plowed field that is ready for the new seed and the new growth. Allow yourself to abide in joy and to be in the place of great wonderment even when you see choices which look to be just the opposite of what you would think they "should" be. Celebrate them and allow yourself to look past the small day-to-day choices to the larger radiance which is you and which will come to be within this reality as you allow this reality to expand.

My peace I give unto you, and even more than that, my excitement I give unto you.

So be it.

Come Unto Me

Beloved one, you have a saying in your Scriptures, an invitation which I extended to you then and extend unto you now and throughout all of time: Come unto me all ye who labor and are heavy laden, and I will give you rest.

Come unto me as you know me to be one Jesus, one Jeshua. Come to me as you would to an elder brother, a friend. Speak with me your troubles, your concerns, as you would do with a friend. Place them in my hands. I will take them. No longer need you be heavy burdened. Come unto me and give me your worries.

Always I stand ready to take from you the illusions of the world. They feel very heavy to you as you are in the midst of dealing with them. Give them to me and I will make them light. Bring them to me, and as much as is possible, leave them in my care and keeping. Now, this will take some practice because you will want to take them back. I have seen you do this: you begin to wrestle with them again. Give them over once again.

My shoulders are broad. My hands are big. I can hold whatever you will give to me. This is what you would do with an elder brother, is it not? One who loves you; one with whom you have conversation; one with whom you have the dialogue that is intimate and loving. You would go to the elder brother, the wise one, and you would say, "This is what is troubling me and I don't know how to get through it. I'm working with it. I have some clues, but it seems very heavy, and of myself I don't know how to go into the future with it." The elder brother lovingly will say, "Let me look at it. Let me take it and work with it." Instantly in that moment the heaviness is lifted from your shoulders.

Beloved one, bring your troubles, your concerns, your challenges to me as one Jeshua. Then come unto Me, the Christ. Bring your problems to the Christ, and in that holy space all will be healed.

Now, how do you do this? At first, it seems easier to understand by coming to a personality. You see each other. You interact with each other as personalities, individuals. You know relationships. It is a step beyond that to bring it to one yet unseen, as you understand me to be. Then come the next step to the Christ.

How do you bring your troubles to the Christ? It begins with the simplicity of the deep breath once again. Whenever you find yourself caught up in the turmoil of the voice of the world, breathe. It is as simple as that to begin the process of remembrance.

Allow yourself then in that space of peace to begin to trust that which is unseen. Have faith in the inner Voice which speaks to you and says, "No matter what is going on, I know that it serves a divine purpose."

When the voice of the world questions what is going to happen in the next day, the next week, the next year, come unto me. Abide with me; me, as you see me to be one Jesus, one Jeshua, for always I welcome your company. Then, more than that, come unto Me, the Christ of you; that place of perfect peace; that place which the world does not understand, and yet the world cannot assail it; that place of perfect wisdom, the inner Kingdom.

Come unto the Christ of you. Walk in the shoes, the sandals of the Christ. Try them on for size. See how they feel. How would it feel to go through an hour, a day as the Christ? "How would I look upon myself? How would everything appear to Me as the Christ?"

Come unto Me, the Christ, and look through the Christ eyes and realize, "I am Christ in this reality having a human experience. It is the Christ of me which allows me to have a human experience."

You have had experiences which were, while you were in the midst of them, most upsetting, most worrisome. You felt even like the body itself was going to be torn asunder because there were so many feelings within yourself. It is called stress. You felt that there was no peace within yourself, no peace within the world, and you have experienced the dark night of the soul that, quite literally, kept you awake all night and would not give you peace.

But as you have looked back upon the experiences, you have seen them in a different light. You could see how all of the events happened in divine order, a catalyst, if you will, for remembrance of the holy Self. Every event, every worrisome time is a catalyst, an opportunity to remember the holy Self and to come up higher. That is why I say, "Come unto Me." Come up higher in your perspective.

Now, the physical eyes will show you separation, and many of the experiences you have known so far have been based upon the physical senses which has led to a reinforcement of the belief that says, "I am separate and I have to defend that which I have. I have to hold on to whatever I have known of security." You run around most busy trying to shore up that which has helped you through in the past, and you have tried to get the friends, the family, the mate, the co-workers to provide your security. Yet the greatest security comes from your flexibility in the face of change. Your true security is found in coming to the Christ. Come unto the Christ of you. Come up higher.

Beloved one, when I say to you, "Come unto me," there are many levels of meaning. Already you have been in process of coming unto me, one Jeshua, one elder brother. Come now unto Me, the Christ, the Christ of you. For, in Truth, the Christ is One and I am not separate from you, nor you from me. We are the Christ. We are the Father in expression having, as you see, a human experience.

In times of struggle come unto Me. In times of questioning, in times when it seems there is much to do and not enough time or not enough energy, times when the voice of the world speaks so loudly that the inner Voice is almost lost, come unto Me. Take the deep breath and return once again to the Home of the Father, that place of perfect peace, the place where it matters not what the outer appearances may be. Come unto Me, abide with Me. I put my arms around you and I take you to my heart, for I love that which you are.

Beloved one, come unto Me.

Oakbridge University Press

Publishers of metaphysical books and materials.

The books that we publish reflect our desire to support and encourage the emerging consciousness of Light and Love, and to assist the awakening of all humanity in Oneness.

Jeshua: The Personal Christ, Volume I

Channeled information from Jeshua ben Joseph — Jesus. We hear about reincarnation, channeling, love, earth changes, ego, the divine feminine, ascension and more. We are reminded of the simplicity and love of Jesus' message to us. Contains a beautiful meditation.

150 pages, paperback $12.95

Jeshua: The Personal Christ, Volume II

Channeled information from Jeshua ben Joseph. Jesus talks about Meditation, The Descent into Matter, Falling in Love, Ascending in Love, The Days to Come, Manifesting, the Age of Enlightenment, Ascension, Prayer and much more. Foreword by Alan Cohen.

There is nothing a human can do on this planet that is more spectacular than to examine the piece of god that resides in themselves. The loving Jeshua material is uplifting and powerful. This really is necessary reading in this new age! — Lee Carroll - Channel for Kryon.

208 pages, paperback $12.95

Jeshua: Speaks: Don't Look for Me in a Tortilla Chip, Volume III

In this volume, Jeshua/Jesus speaks to us about the writings of the Bible more fully. Passages such as the Ten Commandments, The Sermon on the Mount, The Beatitudes take on new and expanded meaning. In a very personal way Jesus describes His baptism and temptations, choosing His disciples and beginning His ministry. "Beloved one, do not seek me in the outer; seek me where I may be found — in your heart."

Mother Mary talks about Holy Communion.

200 pages, paperback $12.95

Jesus and Mastership: The Gospel According to Jesus of Nazareth

Jesus tells His story in His own words. Dictated through the Rev. James C. Morgan, this is the day-to-day account of Jesus' life from age 18, when He went to India to study, through the crucifixion and resurrection. He tells of choosing His disciples, His relationship with Miriam, His ministry and why He taught what He did.

390 pages indexed, paperback $14.95

Yes, I would like to order the following books:
Please send (quantity)

___ Jeshua: The Personal Christ I $12.95

___ Jeshua: The Personal Christ II $12.95

___ Jeshua: Don't look for Me In a Tortilla Chip
              Vol III $12.95

___ Jesus and Mastership $14.95

Please include postage of $2.25 media rate or $4.00 priority mailing for the first book,   plus $1.00 for each additional book.

Enclosed is $_____

Name _____

Address _____

City _____ State ____ Zip _____

Telephone _(____)_____

Visa/Mastercard information:

Account #_____ _____ _____ _____

Expiration Date _____/_____

Signature _____

Oakbridge University Press
4007 Harbor Ridge Rd N.E.
Tacoma, WA 98422

(253) 952-3285   www.oakbridge.org